CULTURES OF THE WORLD
Israel

Cavendish
Square
New York

Published in 2015 by Cavendish Square Publishing, LLC
243 5th Avenue, Suite 136, New York, NY 10016

Library of Congress Cataloging-in-Publication Data

DuBois, Jill.
Israel / by Jill DuBois, Mair Rosh, Josie Elias, and Debbie Nevins.
p. cm. — (Cultures of the world)
Includes index.
ISBN 978-0-76144-995-9 (hardcover) ISBN 978-0-76147-995-6 (ebook)
1. Israel — Juvenile literature. I. DuBois, Jill, 1952-. II. Title.
DS102.95 D82 2015
956.94—d23

Writers, Jill DuBois, Mair Rosh, Josie Elias, Deborah Nevins, third edition
Editorial Director, third edition: Dean Miller
Editor, third edition: Deborah Nevins
Art Director, third edition: Jeffrey Talbot
Designer, third edition: Jessica Nevins
Production Manager, third edition Jennifer Ryder-Talbot
Production Editors: Andrew Coddington and David McNamara
Picture Researcher, third edition: Jessica Nevins

The photographs in this book are used by permission through the courtesy of: Cover photo by dnaveh/Shutterstock.com; ChameleonsEye /Shutterstock.com, 1; Tischenko Irina /Shutterstock.com, 3; Uriel Sinai/Getty Images, 5; ChameleonsEye /Shutterstock.com, 6; ChameleonsEye /Shutterstock.com, 7; Karol Kozlowski /Shutterstock.com, 8; PhotostockAR/Shutterstock.com, 9; maratr/Shutterstock.com, 10; Protasov AN/Shutterstock.com, 12; vvvita/Shutterstock.com, 13; ProfStocker/Shutterstock.com, 14; vblinov/Shutterstock.com, 15; S1001/Shutterstock.com, 16; Anna Liflyand/ File:Herpestes_ichneumon_Египетский_мангуст,_или_фараонова_крыса,_или_ихневмо́н.jpg/Wikimedia Commons, 17; VanderWolf Images/Shutterstock.com, 18; ChameleonsEye /Shutterstock.com, 19; Martin Froyda /Shutterstock.com, 20; sigurcamp/Shutterstock.com, 22; Circle of Juan de la Corte/File:Circle of Juan de la Corte - The Burning of Jerusalem by Nebuchadnezzar's Army - Google Art Project.jpg/Wikimedia Commons, 25; Godot13/File:Israel-2013-Aerial 21-Masada.jpg/Wikimedia Commons, 27; Robert Hoetink/Shutterstock.com, 29; Kurt Strumpf / AP / DAPD, 31; Vince Musi/The White House/File:Bill Clinton, Yitzhak Rabin, Yasser Arafat at the White House 1993-09-13.jpg, 32; Noam Armonn /Shutterstock.com, 36; GALI TIBBON/AFP/Getty Images, 38; ChameleonsEye /Shutterstock.com, 39; ChameleonsEye /Shutterstock.com, 40; pokku/Shutterstock.com, 42; David Silverman/Getty Images, 43; Ariel Jerozolimski/Bloomberg/Getty Images, 45; Gali Tibbon/AFP/Getty Images, 46; Nickolay Vinokurov/Shutterstock.com, 47; ChameleonsEye /Shutterstock.com, 48; Sergei25/Shutterstock.com, 50; Phish Photography/Shutterstock.com, 52; AP Photo/Ariel Schalit, 53; Abbas Momani/AFP/Getty Images, 54; Yuriy Chertok/Shutterstock.com, 55; Lili Rozet Shutterstock.com, 56; ChameleonsEye/Shutterstock.com, 58; Esaias Baitel/Gamma-Rapho/Getty Images, 60; ChameleonsEye/Shutterstock.com, 62; ToskanaINC/Shutterstock.com, 63; ChameleonsEye/Shutterstock.com, 64; ChameleonsEye/Shutterstock.com, 65; JENNY VAUGHAN/AFP/Getty Images, 66; irisphoto1/Shutterstock.com, 67; ChameleonsEye /Shutterstock.com, 68; ChameleonsEye /Shutterstock.com, 69; galaxy67/Shutterstock.com, 71; Yehudit Garinkol/File:PikiWiki Israel 11480 Ben Gurion University.JPG/Wikimedia Commons, 72; ChameleonsEye/Shutterstock.com, 73; AP Photo/Brian Hendler, 74; dnaveh/Shutterstock.com, 75; RickP/File:Kibbutz Barkai panorama 01a.jpg/Wikimedia Commons, 76; ChameleonsEye/Shutterstock.com, 78; Lior Mizrahi/Getty Images, 79; ChameleonsEye/Shutterstock.com, 80; Aleksandar Todorovic/Shutterstock.com, 82; Maksim Dubinsky/Shutterstock.com, 86; djdarkflower/Shutterstock.com, 88; Hitman Sharon/Shutterstock.com, 89; ChameleonsEye /Shutterstock.com, 90; Attila Jandi/Shutterstock.com, 92; ChameleonsEye/Shutterstock.com, 94; gkuna/Shutterstock.com, 96; Godot13/File:Israel-2013(2)-Aerial-Jerusalem-Yad Vashem 01.jpg/Wikimedia Commons, 98; B. Anthony Stewart/National Geographic/Getty Images, 100; maratr/Shutterstock.com, 102; ויטולב ריפכ/File:אנידקר 60.jpg /Wikimedia Commons, 103; David Shankbone/File:Industrial Engineering and Management at Technion by David Shankbone.jpg/Wikimedia Commons, 105; Sergei25/Shutterstock.com, 106; ChameleonsEye /Shutterstock.com, 108; ChameleonsEye /Shutterstock.com, 109; Kobby Dagan/Shutterstock.com, 112; ChameleonsEye/Shutterstock.com, 114; Dan Porges/Photolibrary/Getty Images, 116; ChameleonsEye /Shutterstock.com, 118; ChameleonsEye /Shutterstock.com, 119; p Ryan Rodrick Beiler/Shutterstock.com, 120; Boris-B/Shutterstock.com, 122; ChameleonsEye/Shutterstock.com, 124; James Baigrie/Photolibrary/Getty Images, 125; Kobby Dagan/Shutterstock.com, 127; Tyler Nevins, 130; Tyler Nevins, 131.

Preceding page:
A little girl eats fresh green grapes during the Jewish holiday of Shavuot in Israel.

Printed in the United States of America

CONTENTS

ISRAEL TODAY

ISRAEL IS A VERY SMALL COUNTRY, BUT ITS IMPACT ON THE WORLD IS enormous. It is a tiny Jewish nation surrounded by huge Muslim countries in a part of the world the Muslims consider their own. The conflict that has resulted from this uncomfortable situation expands well beyond Israel's borders and is often an underlying catalyst in many world events.

This conflict is simple on the face of it. To the Jews, Israel is the land promised to them by Yahweh. It is the land of their biblical ancestors, the land that the Jewish people have clung to for thousands of years, even as it was conquered, settled, and ruled by others; and even as they, the Jews themselves, were forced to disperse to other lands. The founding of Israel in 1948 was the realization of a dream that the Jewish people kept alive for more than 2,000 years. For them, it was simply—and finally—a matter of going home again. In Israel, Judaism isn't only a religion; it is a culture, an identity, and a nationality.

To the Palestinians, the Arab people who had been living in what was once called Palestine, Israel is the land that was stolen from them. If that wasn't bad enough, in 1967, Israel went to war against its neighbors and gained more land—from Egypt,

Syria, and Jordan—and ultimately, took more land from the Palestinians. The Palestinians consider themselves to be the indigenous, or native, people of this land. It is the home from which they were forcibly removed. The Palestinian territories that remain—the Gaza Strip, East Jerusalem, and parts of the West Bank region of the Jordan River—are generally considered to be *occupied* by Israel. Some Palestinians say Israel's actions against them are like ethnic cleansing. The Palestinians who remain in Israel complain of discrimination, and have the sense that their country is not their country.

The conflict, therefore, is not simple at all. In fact, it is far more complex than can be explained here. The dispute between the Israelis and the Palestinians overshadows everything else about Israel. Nevertheless, Israelis manage to live normal day-to-day lives. Many Jews and Palestinians get along together just fine, working side by side in some cases. Violence does erupt, because that is part of Israel's story—at least for now—but Israel is not a constant war zone.

Israelis have much to be proud of. They have built a robust democratic society with a dynamic free press and excellent educational and health

An Israeli farmer cares for his crops in Rehovot.

An Israeli family enjoys a picnic on Israel's Independence Day.

facilities. On average, Israel has a high standard of living comparable to that in Western Europe. It has a cutting-edge high-tech industry, a successful agricultural sector, and a strong military. And it enjoys the economic and political support of the United States and other Western nations.

Israelis are enthusiastic citizens. Today, about 73 percent of Israelis are *Sabras*, or Jewish people born in Israel. Of those, almost 39 percent have at least one parent who was also born in Israel. For the most part, Israelis are people who have chosen to live in Israel, or were born to such people. Nationalism runs high. People are proud and excited about this new country that they and their families have built. However, that doesn't mean all Israelis share exactly the same views. Many citizens disagree, and at any given time, there are those who oppose the government, especially as regards the Palestinian situation, and all are free to express their opinions in a nonviolent manner.

Israel is "the Promised Land." It's "the land of milk and honey." It's a sacred land, to Jews, Christians, and Muslims alike. Here, one can pray at the Western

People stand at the 2,000-year-old Western Wall in Jerusalem. Sometimes called the Wailing Wall, it is a place where Jews go to pray.

Wall, trace the steps of Jesus of Nazareth, and visit Islam's third-holiest place of worship. The combination of turbulent politics and holy sites make this a land of contrasts. In Jerusalem, Israel's capital city, ancient walls, shrines, and ruins stand alongside modern office buildings, cafés, and boutiques with the latest international fashions. Beyond Jerusalem, there are brilliant white beaches, enchanting deserts, valleys filled with wildflowers, and a mountain-top ski resort.

For those reasons and many others, people around the world choose Israel as a vacation destination. Tourism is one of Israel's major industries, an important source of money. In 2013, a record high of 3.54 million tourists arrived. Some come for religious reasons, some come to visit families and friends; others come for the arts and culture, the archaeology and ancient history, the resorts, or the natural beauty. Most people come to enjoy a combination of many of those attractions. Jerusalem, one of the oldest cities on Earth, is the country's top attraction. Tel Aviv is considered one of the best beach cities in the world. Other popular sites include Masada, an ancient fortification on a high plateau near the Negev Desert; the Dead Sea; the Sea

The Golden Dome Mosque at the Temple Mount in Jerusalem is sacred to Muslims.

of Galilee; and the coral gardens of the Red Sea.

Jews around the world are promised citizenship here, and thousands of people make *aliyah*, the migration of Jews to Israel, every year. In 2013, about 17,000 people immigrated to their promised land. The largest number, by far, are people from Russia and the other countries of the former Soviet Union; to date, well over a million. In 2012, for example, 7,234 people from former Soviet countries moved to Israel. The next-largest group comes from the United States or Canada with a total of about 138,000; followed by Jews from France, at 79,000. In 2012, the number of people making aliyah from the United States or Canada was 2,525.

For these hundreds of thousands of people, the attraction of living in Israel outweighs the problems. Though some Israelis will admit to being in a constant state of heightened attention, always having an ear cocked for the latest suicide bombing or missile attack—but that is only one layer of their lives. The beauty of residing in this land, combined with a pioneering spirit and stubborn resolve that still pervade Israeli consciousness, make life in Israel today worth living.

GEOGRAPHY

The ruins of Gamla, dating to the first century CE, overlook the Sea of Galilee. The city was built on the top of a steep mountain shaped like a camel's back. *Gamla* means "camel" in Aramaic.

1

ISRAEL IS A YOUNG NATION, FOUNDED in 1948, which is surrounded by angry and offended neighbors—countries that are generally not happy to have this little nation in their part of the world. Because of this, Israel's geographic parameters — its borders, its capital city, and its very right to exist—are in dispute. But Israel is also an ancient land whose mountains, deserts, and bodies of water are described in the Bible. The geographic features of this Israel have remained largely unchanged for thousands of years.

Israel borders Lebanon to the north, Syria to the northeast, Jordan to the east and southeast, and Egypt to the southwest. Israel's southernmost tip extends to the Gulf of Aqaba and the Red Sea.

The country is located in the Middle East, a part of the world that is made up of much of Western Asia and Egypt (which is in Africa). The term "Middle East" was coined in the nineteenth century and reflects a European and American point of view for the region to their east "between Arabia and India."

Israel's position on the eastern shore of the Mediterranean Sea is in a geographic and cultural region that archaeologists and historians call the Levant—the "crossroads of western Asia, the eastern Mediterranean,

The Saar Waterfalls in the Golan Heights flow with snow melt from Mount Herman. The falls are dry in summer and fall.

and northeast Africa." Geographically, Israel is part of the Southern Levant, along with the Palestinian territories, Jordan, and the southern part of Lebanon. Archaeologists often use the term "Southern Levant" to refer to the region in ancient times, but they will also use it as a politically neutral designation for the region today, in which borders are so hotly disputed.

Israel currently consists of some 8,019 square miles (20,770 square km), making it approximately 20 percent smaller than the state of Massachusetts. However, that figure does not include territory Israel captured from Egypt, Syria, and Jordan during the 1967 Six-Day War. Of those territories, the legal status of the Gaza Strip, the West Bank, and the Golan Heights remains a subject of great disagreement among nations. Gaza and the West Bank are claimed by the Palestinians, and Syria claims the Golan Heights. Although Gaza and parts of the West Bank are self governed as Palestinian territory, Israel's authority over these regions is still a matter of dispute. Israel continues to occupy the Golan Heights, but there is no official agreement recognizing it as part of Israel. Therefore, any discussion of this nation's geography is complicated by the world's inability to agree on just what land is—and is not—Israel.

Nevertheless, Israel can be described as a long wedge of land, with its width as narrow as 10 miles (26 km) in some areas and no wider than 70 miles (181 km) at any point. Despite its small size, Israel contains many types of geographical terrain: mountains, valleys, deserts, and forests with a rich variety of plants and animals. Modern-day Jews established themselves mostly on Israel's coastal plain. This narrow strip is about 115 miles (185 km) long and is covered mainly by alluvial soils, which are fertile and suitable for crop cultivation.

TOPOGRAPHY

There are four geographic regions: the hills in the northern and central regions, the coastal plain in the west, the Jordan Rift Valley (part of the Great Rift Valley) in the east, and the Negev Desert in the south.

There are three distinct hilly regions. The hills of Galilee to the north include the highest mountain in Israel, Mount Meron (3,963 feet, or 1,208 m). This range gets a lot of rain and has fertile valleys that produce tobacco and olives. South of the hills of Galilee is the hot, humid, and fertile Esdraelon Plain, formerly a swampland. Upland plateaus lie south of the plain. The western coastal plain is the most populated region with Tel Aviv and the principal port Haifa. This heartland of Israel has citrus plantations, planned settlements, and various industries.

The Great Rift Valley is a deep depression formed millions of years ago when the floor of the Jordan River Valley and the Dead Sea collapsed. It

THE LOWEST POINT ON EARTH

The Dead Sea is a dismal name for a body of water, but it's an accurate one. The water in this saltwater lake evaporates more quickly than fresh water flows into it, making it one of the saltiest bodies of water in the world, with a salt concentration of 33.7 percent. In fact, it's about 9.6 times saltier than the ocean. With such a high level of salinity, the Dead Sea cannot sustain fish or plant life of any kind, and the land around it cannot be cultivated.

Nevertheless, the Dead Sea is a popular place for swimming and bathing. Not only does the water not kill the people who immerse themselves in it, but the water is said to have certain healing qualities. And the density of salt in the water makes the human body very buoyant, so floating on the water is almost effortless.

The Dead Sea is also Earth's lowest place (in a land mass) at 1,401 feet (427 m) below sea level. As well as being a tourist destination, the lake—which is also called the Salt Sea—has great commercial value as one of the world's largest sources of potash. It's also a plentiful source of magnesium bromide, magnesium chloride, and, of course, salt.

The sea is also an historic treasure. It is mentioned in the Bible by several different names, and plays a role in various ancient cultures. It may also be the site of the ancient cities of Sodom and Gomorrah (however, archaeologists disagree about their historical existence). In addition, one of the world's most important archaeological finds was discovered in the rocky hills overlooking this salty sea, and named accordingly—the Dead Sea Scrolls.

extends south approximately 274 miles (710 km) and is dominated by the Jordan River, the Sea of Galilee, and the Dead Sea.

The Negev Desert makes up more than half of Israel's total land area. It was once almost 20 percent larger than it is now, but agricultural

development has decreased its size. The majority of *kibbutzim* (key-BOOT-zim) and *moshavim* (MOH-shau-vim), the agricultural settlements that exist all over Israel, are located in the Negev.

A child wades in the water of Lake Kinneret, also called the Sea of Galilee.

SEAS AND RIVERS

The most important river in Israel is the Jordan River. It originates in the Golan Heights in the north, runs southward near the borders of Lebanon and Syria, through the Sea of Galilee, and empties into the Dead Sea. The Yarkon and Kishon rivers are the only other waterways with permanent flows; others are dry throughout most of the year. The Yarkon River runs into the Mediterranean Sea near Tel Aviv, and the Kishon does so near Haifa. Both the Jordan and the Yarkon are irrigation sources for the Negev Desert.

The National Water Carrier, a freshwater pipeline system from the Sea of Galilee, provides drinking as well as irrigation water to the desert. Also known as Lake Kinneret or Tiberias, the Sea of Galilee is a very popular vacation and fishing area.

The prickly pear, or *sabra*, which is the fruit of a cactus, is the symbol for Israelis.

CLIMATE

The climate of Israel is Mediterranean. The country is located between 29 and 33 degrees latitude north of the Equator, a subtropical region.

The rainy season extends from October to early May, and rainfall peaks in December through February. Rainfall varies considerably by regions from the north to the south. The highest rainfall is observed in the north and center parts of the country, and it decreases in the southern part of Israel, down through the Negev Desert to Eilat where rainfall is negligible. Temperatures differ from north to south as well. In summer, cool breezes prevail in Jerusalem in the north, while the desert can be as hot as 120°F (49°C).

One particularly bothersome part of Israel's weather is its windstorms. Hot desert winds that carry dust and sand can lower humidity and raise temperatures to almost unbearable levels. These windstorms happen occasionally from October to May.

FLORA AND FAUNA

There is great diversity of plant and animal life in Israel, due to the country's location between temperate and tropical zones, bounded by the Mediterranean Sea to the west and desert to the east. Some 2,000 plant species grow here, with wild flowers dotting the mountains and valleys, and cacti adorning the desert. In fact, the native Israeli is known as a *Sabra*, or prickly pear, named after the cactus fruit, which is tough on the outside but sweet on the inside.

Flowers are so plentiful here that the country began selling cut flowers in the 1960s, and in twenty years Israel grew into Europe's largest supplier. Tulips, roses, anemones, irises, poppies, and cyclamen are among the many blooms found in Israel.

For centuries trees covered Israel's mountains, but the demand for lumber and firewood, years of cultivation, and grazing goats and sheep, combined with erosion from the sometimes violent, cyclone-like desert storms, have destroyed much vegetation.

There has been an aggressive and successful reforestation program underway for decades. Millions of trees have been planted under the program. Species of trees and brush that do survive are Aleppo pines and Tabor and evergreen oaks. Almond and fruit trees such as olive, date, and fig are also abundant.

There are several wildlife reserves in Israel, which are mainly inhabited by water birds and smaller animals. These include parts of the region of Arava in the south, Mount Carmel, Mount Meron, and the Hula Lake and marshes in the north. Pelicans, herons, partridges, and varieties of desert and mountain birds are some of the estimated 360 species found in the country.

Wildcats, gazelles, mongooses, jackals, foxes, weasels, wild boars, hares, badgers, and hyenas live in the Jordan River Valley and near the Dead Sea. Snakes and lizards are found in the Negev Desert and other areas with desert-like conditions.

A mongoose prowls the Jordan River Valley.

CITIES

Approximately 90 percent of Israel's 7,821,850 inhabitants live in cities and towns. The three largest cities are Jerusalem (with 815,600 people), Tel Aviv—Jaffa (with 403,700 people), and Haifa (with 265,000 people). A smaller but growing city in the south is Beersheba (with 197,300 people). Other urban centers include Netanya, Eilat, Hebron, Rehovot, Ashdod, and Shechem.

JERUSALEM

Jerusalem is the capital of the Jewish state (although some groups dispute this). Most foreign governments, however, maintain their embassies in Tel Aviv. Like many cities with pasts that span the ages, Jerusalem is a fascinating mixture of old and new.

Jerusalem is a holy city for three distinct religions—a truth that makes the city exciting and significant, but also prone to conflict. It has been the

The view from the Mount of Olives looks out on the Old City of Jerusalem.

historical, spiritual, and national center of the Jewish people since King David proclaimed it the capital of the land in 1000 BCE. In addition to its importance for the Jews, the city holds great significance for Christians and Muslims. For Christians, it is the site of Jesus' crucifixion, burial, and resurrection. For Muslims, it is the site of El-Aqsa Mosque, Islam's third-holiest shrine.

Tel Aviv has beautiful white sand beaches on the Mediterranean Sea.

TEL AVIV-JAFFA

Tel Aviv, which means "hill of spring," was founded in 1909 by a group of European immigrants living in the town of Jaffa, a neighboring seaport. Jaffa grew rapidly within a short time and is characteristic of the fast pace that still exists there today. Tel Aviv united with Jaffa to become one city more than fifty years ago. Because of the melding of the two cities, the Tel Aviv—Jaffa area is also an interesting combination of old and new.

Tel Aviv is the most cosmopolitan of Israel's cities. It is home to many foreign embassies and boasts numerous theater groups and museums. There are beautiful white beaches that hug the blue waters of the Mediterranean Sea. As a modern metropolis, however, Tel Aviv also suffers the problems of other big cities, including traffic jams, urban poverty, and development problems.

Jaffa, on the other hand, is one of the world's oldest cities. Its name is said to be derived from Japeth, son of Noah, who built the town. Jaffa has the legendary port from which the biblical prophet Jonah set sail before being consumed by a great fish. In Jaffa today there are open markets and old forts that were built in the tenth century BCE.

Jaffa retains its Eastern character, perhaps because thousands of Israel's North African and Asian Jews reside here. The narrow alleys and streets are

For much of modern history, Jerusalem has been divided into two parts, the Jordanian and Israeli sectors. After 1967 the entire city came under Israel's control. Today there are still two Jerusalems—the Old City and the New City.

THE OLD CITY *in the eastern part of Jerusalem has been besieged by numerous wars since ancient times. The Six-Day War of 1967 reunited the two parts of Jerusalem, which had been divided by the 1948 war, under Israeli rule.*

Seven gates provide entrance to the ancient walled city. Inside, there are five sections: the revived Jewish Quarter, with its fragmented historical remains; the Christian Quarter, with the Church of the Holy Sepulchre, which is believed to be the site of the crucifixion and burial of Jesus; the Armenian Quarter, which has a residential area with ancient buildings, churches,

and chapels; and the densely populated Muslim Quarter, with the ancient temple area, the Temple Mount, the Western Wall, and the eight-sided Dome of the Rock, where Muslims believe the Prophet Muhammad ascended to heaven.

The Temple Mount, with its importance to Jews and Muslims alike, remains one of Jerusalem's most troublesome spots. The Old City has been declared a protected cultural monument by UNESCO, a department of the United Nations.

THE NEW CITY *itself is not as spectacular as the Old City, and the name is misleading because parts of it are very old. It has many areas of great religious significance, including the Garden of Gethsemane, where Jesus prayed before he was arrested and crucified; the Mount of Olives with its ancient Jewish cemetery; and Mount Zion and King David's tomb. It also has office towers, high-rises, wide streets, and lovely parks.*

Jerusalem is the focal point of the Jewish people's national and spiritual life. It is the seat of the parliament, or Knesset (kuh-NESS-et), and home to the Hebrew University. The National Museum and important government and commercial institutions are also located here.

Jerusalem has two very distinct features. All of its older buildings are made of Jerusalem stone, which gives the city a uniform look. Also, the city has a special fragrance, known as "Jerusalem perfume," which is actually the scent of wildflowers that wafts through the air in the evening. This lovely aroma disappears when it is burned off with the morning sun.

home to many artists, and among their stalls are outdoor cafés and beautiful antique shops. The port, said to be one of the oldest in the world, served as an entry point to thousands of Jews who came to start a new life. Its harbor is now closed to commercial shipping and has given way to Haifa as the new economic port.

HAIFA

Haifa has existed since the third century, but its main period of growth did not occur until the twentieth century. The establishment of the Haifa-Damascus Railway led to development of Haifa's harbor by the British in 1929. It remains Israel's major Mediterranean port.

Israel's heavy-industry center is also in the Haifa area. Petroleum refineries, automobile and tire manufacturers, glass factories, cement works, steel mills, fertilizer producers, and shipbuilders are all located here. Even though it has a prosperous industrial focus, Haifa is a splendid city whose beauty has been compared to that of San Francisco. It is also the world center for the Baha'i faith.

INTERNET LINKS

www.goisrael.com
The site of the Israel Ministry of Tourism offers a wide range of information about the land. Click on "Regions and Destinations."

geography.howstuffworks.com/oceans-and-seas/dead-sea-dead.htm
How Stuff Works: "Is the Dead Sea Really Dead?"
An in-depth article on the science of the Dead Sea.

www.jerusalem.muni.il/jer_main/defaultnew.asp?lng=2
The official site of the city of Jerusalem offers history, photo galleries, and more.

HISTORY

The City of David is the birthplace of Jerusalem. It is where King David established his kingdom in 1004 BCE, and where the People of Israel were united under his rule. Today the ruins are part of an archaeological park.

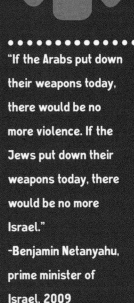

2

HISTORY IS IMPORTANT TO ANY country, but perhaps none more so than Israel. Its history defines its identity and character. The roots of the Israeli people, their religions, and their nation's very reason for being go back hundreds and thousands of years.

The history of the Land of Israel, as this region has been referred to since biblical times, is inextricably related to that of the Jewish people. It is a blending of national and religious traditions dating to the era of the biblical patriarchs Abraham, Isaac, and Jacob. The Bible serves as the principal source for stories chronicling the events of ancient Israel, though modern archaeologists and scholars attempt to pin down the veracity of those stories with historical evidence.

Yet the modern State of Israel was only founded in 1948. Because of its prime location at the crossroads of Europe, Africa, and Asia, this land was always the target of conquerors.

EARLY HISTORY

Israel's history is said to have begun around 1800 BCE with the westward migration of a group of nomadic herdsmen from Mesopotamia (today's Iraq). They were led, according to the Bible, by Abraham, who is considered the father of Judaism. Setting up tents and digging wells, they settled in Canaan (Palestine's former name). These people wandered around Canaan for about three generations, until a famine forced them to migrate once again.

Abraham's grandson Jacob (also known as Israel) relocated with his twelve sons and their families to Egypt. These families grew in numbers and formed twelve tribes, collectively known as the Israelites. The tribes remained in the Nile Delta region for several centuries, and the Egyptian pharaohs eventually enslaved them.

Around 1300 BCE, according to the traditional narrative, the prophet Moses led the Israelites out of Egypt and slavery. They crossed the Red Sea and wandered around the Sinai Peninsula between Palestine and Egypt. After weeks or months of traveling in the desert, the Israelites arrived at Mount Sinai and made a covenant, or sacred agreement, to worship only one God and to follow his laws, the Ten Commandments. For forty years, Moses educated the Israelites and laid the foundation of the community.

Around 1250 BCE, the twelve tribes returned to Canaan under the guidance of Joshua, who succeeded Moses. They encountered the Philistines, who had recently been forced from their homeland of Crete, and the Canaanites, who did not want the Israelites to settle there. For the next 200 years, these three groups fought for Canaan.

The Canaanites were defeated by the Israelites around 1125 BCE. The Philistines, however, had a superior military organization and better weapons. In around 1050 BCE, they defeated the Israelites, causing the twelve tribes to unite for strength under one king. Under Saul, however, there was dissension that continued until his death. David succeeded Saul and was able to unite the armies to defeat the Philistines and take over Canaan.

David established Jerusalem as the capital of the kingdom of Israel and began building the city. Upon his death, his son Solomon became king and completed the city and the First Temple of Jerusalem in which the Israelites could worship God. However, after Solomon's death, the different tribes began feuding, and they split the kingdom into two parts—Israel, with its capital at Samaria in the north, was home to ten tribes, and Judah, with its capital at Jerusalem in the south, was home to the remaining two tribes. Citizens of the southern portion became known as the Jewish people.

Over the next few centuries, the two Hebrew kingdoms fought each other while at the same time tried to fend off attacks from outsiders.

UNDER FOREIGN RULE

In the early eighth century BCE, the Assyrians from the north attacked and conquered Israel, exiling some Jews and taking others as slaves. Around 597 BCE, the Babylonians, under their king Nebuchadnezzar, came and conquered Judah and destroyed the temple in Jerusalem. Many Jews were exiled to the Babylonian Empire, in what today is Iraq.

Nebuchadnezzar's army burns Jerusalem in the year 597 BCE in this painting by Juan de la Corte (1580-1663).

The Jews were freed less than fifty years later when Cyrus the Great of Persia (today's Iran) conquered the Babylonians. Cyrus allowed the Jews to return to their homeland and rebuild the temple. In return, Israel remained under the control of the Persians for another two centuries.

In 332 BCE the Persian Empire collapsed after being attacked by Alexander the Great of Macedonia. Alexander allowed self-government and religious freedom for the Jews. Later, the Ptolemies of Egypt and the Seleucids of Syria succeeded Alexander for control of the region. Eventually, the Seleucids tried to impose their Greek religion on the Jews. But under the guidance of a warrior named Judah Maccabee, the Jews revolted. Although Judah died, the Jews reestablished their independence in 141 BCE after prolonged fighting.

Less than a century later, however, the Romans occupied the Jewish state. The land became a part of the Roman Empire in 63 BCE, when it was renamed Judea. Over the next century, the Jews clashed with the Roman rulers, for they wanted to maintain their own religion and independence. Spurred on by a group known as the Zealots, the Jews launched the Great Revolt against the Romans. In the process, the Romans destroyed Jerusalem and the Second Temple in 70 CE, leaving all but the Western Wall in ruins.

In 132 CE, Simon Bar Kokhba led Jewish fighters against the Roman Empire for about three years before being crushed. To ensure that the Jews would not rise again, the Roman emperor Hadrian built a Roman city on the site of

Jerusalem and called it Aelia Capitolina. He built a temple to the Roman god Jupiter on the site of the Temple of Jerusalem. The Romans did not allow the Jews to enter the city, and deported the Jews to colonies around the world.

This scattering, known as the Diaspora, sent most of the Jews to the shores of the Black Sea, the Greek Islands, and the coasts of the Mediterranean Sea. Some Jews fled to northern Europe and areas eastward. Regardless of where they settled, the Jews clung to their religious and cultural roots, one day hoping to return to their land.

THE FIGHT FOR PALESTINE

Palestine remained under Roman rule for the next 500 years. During that time, Christianity gained importance, as followers of Jesus of Nazareth spread his gospel. Meanwhile, Muhammad ibn 'Abd Allah was born in what today is Saudi Arabia, and by the time of his death in 632 CE, he had founded a new religion which would sweep the lands of the Middle East and beyond. That religion was Islam.

After the fall of the Western Roman Empire in 476, the Eastern Roman Empire, or Byzantine Empire, continued. These rulers did not take the rise of Islam seriously and underestimated the Arab military. In 638 the Arabs attacked and conquered Jerusalem. For the next 460 years, the country remained under Islamic rule. Some exiled Jews returned to Palestine during this time.

The early years of Arab rule were acceptable to the Jews, but later, the Muslim spiritual rulers introduced restrictions such as heavy taxes on non-Muslims. At this time, because of Jerusalem's importance to Christianity, soldiers from Europe launched a crusade to take the land back from Muslim rule. In 1099 the Crusaders conquered Jerusalem and ruled most of Palestine for eighty-eight years.

In 1187 a Muslim army under Saladin recaptured Jerusalem. After Saladin's death, the Christians regained Jerusalem, but only until 1291, when the Egyptian Mamluks returned Muslim rule to Palestine for the next 225 years. During this time, increasing numbers of Jews returned to the Holy Land. By 1517 the Mamluks had been overthrown by the Ottoman, or Turkish, Empire.

In 70 CE, after Jerusalem fell to the Romans, resistance fighters known as the Zealots took refuge on a rugged mountain named Masada. The mountain, which overlooks the Dead Sea, forms a natural fortress. At the top, the Judean king Herod the Great, who reigned from 37 BCE to 4 CE, had earlier built a palace complex in classical Roman style.

A Roman army of 15,000 arrived to fight this Jewish force of fewer than 1,000. But it took them almost two years to break through Masada's protective wall.

Realizing that they were outnumbered and that, at the very best, a life of slavery was all that was in store for them, the Zealots committed suicide rather than be captured. Under the leadership of Eleazar Ben Jair, the remaining 960 Jews organized and carried out a mass suicide to ensure a hollow victory for the Romans.

Masada remained largely untouched for more than thirteen centuries. Once it was finally discovered and identified, it underwent extensive archaeological digs in the 1960s. Bones unearthed at the site went through radiocarbon dating tests, which determined that the skeletons are probably those of the Jewish rebels who killed themselves rather than surrender to the Romans.

Today Masada is maintained as a national park by the government of Israel and is protected by the country's 1978 Antiquities Law. In 2001, the United Nations Educational, Scientific, and Cultural Organization (UNESCO), named Masada as a World Heritage site, saying, "Masada [is] a symbol both of Jewish cultural identity and, more universally, of the continuing human struggle between oppression and liberty."

The Ottomans removed all Mamluk administrators, divided Palestine into districts, and allowed the Jewish community to expand. At this time, the vast majority of the population was of Arabic lineage and was spread out over all of Palestine. In contrast, the Jews tended to create pockets of settlements.

Over the next 300 years, Jewish colonies grew, and Jews from Europe and the Far East migrated to Palestine. By the end of the nineteenth century, the dream of reestablishing a homeland had begun to take shape.

ESTABLISHING A HOMELAND

Several historical events helped establish the Israeli homeland. The movement to create a Jewish state became known as Zionism. In the later part of the nineteenth century, Jews began buying up plots of land in Ottoman Palestine. They set up communities, farms, and the first modern Jewish village.

Around that time, oppression of Jews in Eastern Europe was growing. In Russia, Jews were being persecuted. Waves of anti-Jewish riots called *pogroms* swept Russia from 1881 to 1884. During these rampages, rioters destroyed Jewish houses and properties, and the Russian Jews were frightened and alarmed. Thousands of Jews left their homes in eastern Europe and Russia in search of safety. Many immigrated to the United States. About 15,000 to 25,000 Jews fled to Palestine, the land of their ancient ancestors. This immigration was called the First Aliyah.

In 1896, Theodor Herzl wrote *The Jewish State*, a book in which he suggested that Jews return to Palestine from countries where they were being persecuted. One year later, the World Zionist Organization was established. Herzl's efforts inspired the Second Aliyah in 1904. Waves of immigrants entered Palestine after that and formed agricultural settlements throughout the country.

During World War I, British Foreign Secretary Arthur Balfour declared that his government favored "the establishment in Palestine of a national home for the Jewish people." Shortly after, British forces defeated the Ottoman Empire and captured Palestine. In the aftermath of World War I, the Ottoman Empire was broken up, new countries were established, national boundaries shifted, old governments were dismantled and new ones set up. A whole new map of the world emerged, with much of the region under British rule.

By this time, the Arabs also wanted independence. They saw the fall of the Ottoman Empire as the opportunity for them to claim Palestine as their own, regardless of what the British government proposed. Despite the promise

At the end of World War I in 1918, the victorious Allied nations (Great Britain, France, and Italy) blamed Germany for starting the war. They, along with the United States, devised a peace treaty, called the Treaty of Versailles, that severely punished Germany. The settlement left many Germans humiliated and bitter. This resentful national mood turned against the European Jews, who were blamed for the war as well as its aftermath. Germany was deeply in debt and its people were starving. All of this enabled Adolf Hitler and the Nazi Party to take power in Germany.

Hitler set out to conquer Europe, which triggered World War II in 1939. He also aimed to purge the continent of its Jews. In that, he largely succeeded. By 1945, Hitler's Nazis had killed two out of every three European Jews—some six million men, women, and children—in what came to be called the Holocaust.

In 1945 the United States, Great Britain, and the other Allies finally defeated Germany. The shocking crimes against the Jews elicited worldwide sympathy and support for the creation of a Jewish homeland. Many European Jews with nowhere to go entered Palestine. By 1946, the Jewish population there had grown to nearly 500,000.

A pile of shoes worn by people who were killed in Auschwitz during the Holocaust.

that the civil and religious rights of Arabs and Jews would be safeguarded, the roots of conflict were established. The British would rule over Palestine until 1948.

Between 1919 and 1933, the number of Jews in Palestine more than tripled to 200,000. As more Jewish oppression and persecution took place in Europe, Arab aggression against Palestinian Jews also increased, and the Arabs revolted against British control. By 1937 the British decided that dividing the land was the best solution, but they limited the number of Jews that could settle in Israel and proposed the start of Arab and Jewish states within ten years.

INDEPENDENCE

After the war, the question of Palestine came up again. Since they could satisfy neither side, the British placed the issue of dividing the land with the United Nations before leaving the region. The United Nations voted in favor of Palestine being divided into separate Arab and Jewish states, with Jerusalem having special international status. The Arabs rejected the plan. On May 14, 1948, Israel declared itself an independent state.

Within twenty-four hours of the British leaving the land, the combined forces of Lebanon, Jordan, Egypt, Syria, and Iraq attacked Israel. The Israeli defense troops fought with the help of donations from foreign nations and individuals. After months of fighting, a peace treaty was signed in January 1949. Israel had gained 50 percent more land than it had been given, as well as half of Jerusalem. The Arab nations, meanwhile, imposed an economic boycott on Israel.

The first Israeli elections were held after the ceasefire, with Chaim Weizmann elected president and David Ben-Gurion prime minister. The new government was admitted into the United Nations in May 1949.

THE SIX-DAY WAR

Clashes with Syria at the eastern border started in the 1960s. When Israel threatened to fight back, Syria enlisted the help of Egypt. On June 5, 1967, Israel simultaneously attacked Egypt, Syria, and Jordan. It took only six days for the Israeli army to totally defeat its enemies in what came to be called the Six-Day War. After the ceasefire, Israel had increased its land size by nearly 200 percent, conquering the Golan Heights, the Sinai Peninsula, and the West Bank of the Jordan River, plus all of Jerusalem. After the war, the Palestine Liberation Organization (PLO) stepped up its attacks on Israel and Jews. These included terrorist acts, such as hijacking airplanes of innocent civilians.

THE MUNICH MASSACRE

In 1972, the Summer Olympics were held in Munich, West Germany. (At the time, Germany was divided into two countries, West Germany and East Germany.) Security was very light; the Germans wanted the competition to have a friendly, open atmosphere. On September 5, during the second week of the Games, eight Palestinian terrorists kidnapped eleven members of the Israeli delegation—five athletes, two referees, and four coaches. The terrorists were members of Black September, a shadowy faction of the Palestine Liberation Organization, then headed by Yasser Arafat.

The terrorists demanded the release of some 200 Arab prisoners being held by Israel. But Israel, led by Prime Minister Golda Meir, not only refused to release the prisoners, but refused to negotiate with the terrorists at all, according to its policy. The West German government, however, did negotiate, stalling for time while it planned a rescue operation. After a day filled with appalling errors in judgment by the German officials, and sloppy police work, the terrorists killed all of the Israeli hostages. Five of the Palestinian gunmen were killed and three were captured.

The long aftermath of the Munich Massacre is almost as shocking and dramatic as the event itself, as Israel set out to exact justice and shut down the terrorists. One result of the event is that governments worldwide immediately created anti-terrorism units. And ever since that dreadful day, the Olympic Committee takes security very seriously.

THE YOM KIPPUR WAR

On October 6, 1973, hoping to win back territory lost to Israel in the 1967 war, Syria and Egypt attacked Israel. The surprise assault began on Yom Kippur, the most solemn of Jewish holy days. Caught off guard, Israel suffered great losses but eventually managed to beat back the attack. On October 25, Egypt and Israel signed a cease-fire agreement.

Although that war was short-lived, Israelis were critical of Prime Minister

Golda Meir for allowing the country to be so vulnerable. Meir stepped down as president a few months later, in April 1973. Israel also realized, after this war, that a peace treaty with Egypt would be a desirable goal.

Sporadic clashes continued, however, and in 1975 an interim agreement was signed to bring about Israel's withdrawal from the Sinai Peninsula. A United Nations peacekeeping force was put in place between Israel and Egypt.

THE CAMP DAVID ACCORDS

Israel Prime Minister Menachem Begin and PLO leader Yasser Arafat shake hands in 1993, the year of the peace accord in Oslo. President Bill Clinton looks on.

A breakthrough in the peace process came in 1977 when Egyptian President Anwar el-Sadat stated his willingness to meet with Israeli leaders. In 1978 U.S. President Jimmy Carter met with Sadat and Israeli Prime Minister Menachem Begin at Camp David, the president's retreat in Maryland. The thirteen days of secret negotiations, while difficult, resulted in a two-part agreement called the Camp David Accords. One of the agreements led directly to the Israeli-Egypt Peace Treaty in 1979. It spelled out Israel's complete withdrawal from the Sinai Peninsula and eventual Arab self-rule in the West Bank and the Gaza Strip. It was the first peace treaty between Israel and an Arab nation.

As a result of the Camp David Accords, Sadat and Begin were honored with the 1978 Nobel Peace Prize. In 1981, Sadat was assassinated by extremists in Egypt who were enraged that he had made peace with Israel.

THE FIRST INTIFADA

In 1987, Palestinians in Gaza rioted, causing general civil disobedience and unrest (known as an *intifada*) throughout Israel's occupied territories. A year later, the PLO declared itself an independent state. The PLO also recognized Israel's right to exist, a condition required by the United States before it would acknowledge the PLO. This move prompted the United States to start low-level peace talks between Israel and the PLO.

HURDLES ON THE ROAD TO PEACE

The conflict between Israel and the Palestinians is deeply rooted and extremely complicated. The best attempts at establishing a lasting peace have met seemingly insurmountable obstacles. Some of the key sticking points are:

Israel's right to exist. *Many Arabs argue that Israel was established on Palestinian lands and it is an illegal state because Arab leaders and governments did not agree to the 1947 United Nations Partition Plan for Palestine. Those Arab leaders who are willing to grant Israel's right to exist nevertheless dispute its borders.*

Israel asserts its right to exist based on biblical evidence; the continued presence of Jews in the region over centuries; the 1917 British Balfour Declaration, supporting a homeland for the Jewish people; the persecution of the Jews in other countries, especially the Holocaust; and the U.N. partition plan.

Israel's borders. *Many Arab leaders insist that Israel return to its original pre-1967 borders. Israel captured land in the 1967 Six-Day War, including the Golan Heights, a section in the north that had been part of Syria; the West Bank of the Jordan River, a Palestinian area; and the Gaza Strip, a 25-mile (41-km) long coastal section on the Mediterranean bordering Egypt.*

Settlements. *Jewish settlers have built new communities, or outposts, in the occupied territories that Israel captured in the 1967 war. Much of the international community regards these settlements as illegal encroachments on Palestinian lands. Palestinians complain the Jewish settlements are part of a plan to slowly take over all of the Palestinian territories.*

Jerusalem. *Both Israel and the Palestinians claim Jerusalem as their capital city.*

The Law of Return, The Right of Return. *The 1950 Israeli Law of Return states that Israel was established as a Jewish homeland, and therefore all Jews and their families have the right to immigrate to Israel. This right does not extend to the Palestinians. The Palestinians say the "right of return" is a principle guaranteed by international law, which states that refugees have the right to return to their country of origin. Palestinians claim to be refugees from the original establishment of Israel, which forced them from their homes.*

Violence. *Some Palestinians view suicide attacks and missile launches as a justified means of dealing with an occupying force. Israelis view such acts as terrorism and believe they have the right to protect themselves against such attacks.*

In September 1993, Israel and the PLO signed a peace accord in Oslo, Norway. It stipulated that Israel would grant the Palestinians self-government in the Gaza Strip and the West Bank town of Jericho. This agreement was honored in May 1994, when Israel withdrew from Jericho and Gaza. In 2000, U.S. President Bill Clinton brought PLO Chairman Yasser Arafat and Israeli Prime Minister Ehud Barak together at Camp David to pursue further peace talks. However, the talks failed and nothing came of them. However, frustration and anger did result, and in 2001, a second intifada erupted.

THE SECOND INTIFADA

This uprising was even more violent and deadly than the first. Hard-liners on both sides denounced the Oslo agreement—Israelis objected to the withdrawal of their forces from Gaza, and the Palestinians decried the assertion of Israel's right to exist. A new terror phenomenon emerged: Palestinian suicide bombers killed dozens of Israeli citizens. The Israeli military response killed many Palestinians. The revolt lasted about five years, and the death toll is estimated at 3,000 Palestinians and 1,000 Israelis.

In 2005 Israel completed its withdrawal from Gaza, giving that tiny coastal strip over to the Palestinians. Meanwhile, the Palestinians themselves were in conflict, with the old, secular PLO facing opposition from a new Islamist group called Hamas (Islamic Resistance Movement). Since 2007, Hamas has governed the Gaza Strip. The United States, Great Britain, and some other Western nations consider Hamas to be a terrorist organization.

Although Israel ended its military occupation of Gaza, the U.N. and certain other international groups say Israel is still an occupying force over the Gaza Strip. This assertion is based on Israel's continuing control of the Strip's airspace and territorial waters, which allows Israel to control the movement of people and goods in or out of Gaza by air or sea. Israel disagrees and maintains that it is out of Gaza.

Since Hamas took over government of the Palestinian territories in 2007, thousands of rockets have been continuously fired at Israel from Gaza, killing hundreds of civilians. In 2008, a 22-day war broke out between Israel and Gaza which killed more than 1,000 Palestinians and caused a tremendous amount of damage to the small territory. In addition, Israel set up a blockade around Gaza to block its access to imported weaponry. The blockades also seriously hurt the region's economy and its population of more than 1.6 million Palestinians.

Israel and the Palestinians renewed peace talks in 2013, aided in their negotiations by a U.S. team. In March 2014, as the peace talks appeared to be in danger of collapse, U.S. Secretary of State John Kerry flew to Israel to meet with Prime Minister Netanyahu and Palestinian President Mahmoud Abbas. However, several issues prevented the talks from achieving success.

"Israel cannot be expected to negotiate with a gun to its head."
–Israeli president Benjamin Netanyahu, 2014

INTERNET LINKS

news.bbc.co.uk/2/hi/middle_east/7385661.stm
BBC News, "History of Israel: Key Events"
A video timeline from 1948—2008 of key events in the nation's history.

www.thejewishmuseum.org/archaeologytimeline
The Jewish Museum of New York
A timeline of ancient Israel from 1200 BCE to 499 CE.

www.simpletoremember.com/articles/a/what-the-fight-in-israel-is-all-about/
"What the Fight in Israel Is All About: Why are Israel and Palestine fighting?"
An explanation of the conflict from a Jewish-Israeli point of view.

middleeastvoices.voanews.com/2012/11/quicktake-the-gaza-conflict-a-palestinian-perspective-42440
Middle East Voices: The Gaza Conflict — A Palestinian Perspective
An interview with Palestinian diplomat Maen Rashid Areikat.

whc.unesco.org/en/list/1040
UNESCO World Heritage
Photos, history, and an explanation of the site's importance.

GOVERNMENT

A young Israeli holds the country's blue and white flag.

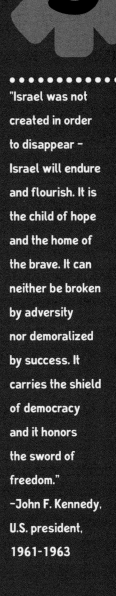

3

AMONG ITS OTHER DISTINCTIONS, Israel has been called the only free country in the Middle East and North Africa. Freedom House, an independent watchdog organization that analyzes the political and civil liberties of governments worldwide, has awarded the rating "Free" to Israel every year since the ranking began in 1972. In 2014, no other country in the region achieved that status.

Israel is a parliamentary democracy with a unicameral (one-house) legislature, or parliament. This legislature—known as the Knesset—along with the prime minister and the cabinet are responsible for governing Israel.

The president is the head of state, elected by the parliament to a five-year term. The president's role is mainly ceremonial, similar to that of the reigning monarch of the United Kingdom. Israel's president has little political power, except to grant pardons and appoint judges to the Supreme Court.

The president also appoints ambassadors and the state comptroller, who oversees budgets and the functions of all public bodies, and performs moral and educational functions. All residents of Israel are eligible to be presidential candidates.

"Israel was not created in order to disappear – Israel will endure and flourish. It is the child of hope and the home of the brave. It can neither be broken by adversity nor demoralized by success. It carries the shield of democracy and it honors the sword of freedom."
–John F. Kennedy, U.S. president, 1961-1963

THE KNESSET

The Knesset has 120 members who are elected for a maximum of four years; the 120 seats are given in direct ratio to the popular vote. Voters do not elect individuals, but political parties and subsequently the candidates they support. The more votes a party gets, the more seats it wins in the parliament.

Canada Prime Minister Stephen Harper addresses the Knesset in Jerusalem on January 20, 2014.

No party has ever achieved a clear majority in the history of Israeli politics. The system is often criticized because voters have little control over the individuals who obtain these critical seats. However, those who support the system point out that it forces people to vote on issues rather than people.

The Knesset conducts business in a way similar to the British House of Commons, and its voting system is like the ones used in France and Germany. It has unlimited legislative authority, and enactments cannot be vetoed by the prime minister, president, or Supreme Court. The Knesset holds two sessions each year. The winter sessions opens after the High Holy Days, and the summer session opens after Independence Day on May 14.

BASIC LAWS

The Jewish state has no formal constitution, only a set of basic laws that were enacted with the intention that they would eventually become part of a constitution.

In the early years of statehood, Israeli lawmakers tried to compose a formal document. However, no agreement could be reached. So in 1950 the Knesset decided to gradually acquire a constitution, with the resolution stating that it would grow "chapter by chapter in such a way that each chapter will by itself constitute a fundamental law."

By the late 1980s, there were nine basic laws. These involve areas such as the function of the Knesset, the definition of Israel's borders, the role of the president, the operation of the government, the state economy, the army, the judiciary, elections, and Jerusalem.

There is no procedure to change the laws, although the Knesset can start a new government by simply getting a majority vote. But this is not likely to happen because the government is devoted to a rich tradition of democracy and the exchange of political ideas.

THE JUDICIAL SYSTEM

The judicial structure is composed of three courts: civil, religious, and military. Crime is handled by the civil court; marriage and divorce are administered by the religious court; and military matters are overseen by the military court.

Before taking office, judges must pledge allegiance to the state of Israel and take an oath to be neutral and just at all times. In addition, all judges, except those in the religious court, must vow loyalty to the laws of the state.

Israeli laws are borrowed from many areas, including Ottoman and British laws. Special investigative panels have been formed for unusual cases or situations.

The Supreme Court hears appeals from civil and criminal cases. It also hears cases that do not fall directly under the authority of the other courts. The number of justices that make up the Supreme Court is determined by the Knesset. In recent years, there have been fourteen justices; a minimum of three must be present to hold a court session. In 2004, Salim Jubran was selected as the first Arab to hold a permanent appointment as a Supreme Court Justice.

Shimon Peres served four times as Israel's prime minister. In 1994, he was awarded the Nobel Peace Prize, along with Yitzak Rabin and Yasser Arafat, for producing the Oslo agreement.

The Supreme Court is the principal guardian of fundamental rights in Israel and protects individuals from unfair or wrong practices by public agencies and officials. It has authority in almost all areas of Israeli life and it serves almost like a formal constitution. Many Israelis consider the Supreme Court the guardian of democracy.

RELIGIOUS COURTS

Religious courts in Israel have authority over personal matters such as marriage, divorce, alimony, and religious wills of members of a religious community. Each major religious community has its own courts, deciding on all matters of their members' personal status and problems. If people of different religions are involved in a legal dispute, the president of the Supreme Court determines which court will have authority.

Benjamin Netanyahu became prime minister of Israel in 2009.

District courts can also have authority in personal legal matters if all parties involved agree on their participation.

Within the state of Israel, there are Jewish Rabbinical Courts, Muslim Courts, Christian Courts, and Druze Courts.

THE CABINET

The cabinet, consisting of the prime minister and a number of other ministers, is Israel's central political power and the top policy-making body. The prime minister must be a member of the Knesset, but this is not required of the other cabinet ministers. The Knesset confirms the cabinet after the prime minister submits a list of names and a detailed report of the policies and fundamental principles of the cabinet.

The cabinet can be dissolved if the prime minister dies, if the Knesset officially reprimands it—known as "passing a censure"—or if it resigns as a group. Individuals can resign from the cabinet without disbanding it, but if the prime minister resigns, the whole cabinet must go with him or her.

Cabinet posts are divided among the various political parties, or coalitions of the smaller ones, usually in proportion to the strength of the various parties.

LOCAL GOVERNMENT

Israel is divided into six administrative districts, each of which has a commissioner. Towns and cities with more than 20,000 people are run by municipal corporations, whereas smaller towns are run by local councils. Villages are collectively administered by regional councils.

There are seventy-five Israeli municipalities granted "city" status by the Ministry of the Interior. There are 265 local councils, and fifty-four regional councils representing 700 villages, some of which are mainly Druze or Arab. All local government leaders are chosen through elections.

The local government provides basic services such as water supply, drainage, roads, parks, and social assistance, as well as sports, cultural, health, and educational facilities. To provide such services, the local government gets funds from a municipal tax, where the rates and budgets are authorized by the Ministry of the Interior.

INTERNET LINKS

www.gov.il/firstgov/english
The Israel government portal has history, facts, and a list of government officials.

www.mfa.gov.il
The Israel Ministry of Foreign Affairs.

www.knesset.gov.il
The Knesset
The official website explains the workings and history of the Knesset and lists its members by party.

ECONOMY

This view of the Valley of Jezreel shows fertile fields and stocked fish ponds.

STRAWBERRIES BLOOM IN ISRAEL. So do oranges, lemons, and grapefruits—and plumegranates, pomelits, lamoon plums, pita peaches, nectarine-mangoes, black tomatoes, and nano watermelons. Those oddly named fruits are some of the new hybrid species recently developed in Israel.

A worker at the Hazera Genetics lab in Israel sorts the tiny seeds of a hybrid cherry tomato called Summer Sun, which the company developed. These valuable seeds are worth more than their weight in gold and the blue tint is a company trademark.

4

"We do not rejoice in victories. We rejoice when a new kind of cotton is grown and when strawberries bloom in Israel."
–Golda Meir, prime minister of Israel, 1969-1974

Israel exports more than $2 billion worth of produce. Citrus fruits, bananas, melons, and tomatoes are some of its major crops. Potatoes, peppers, carrots, and apples are other important products. Israel is also among the world's top developers of new varieties—fruits and vegetables that are better tasting, more disease resistant and nutritious, and produce higher yields.

Israel grows enough food to feed its people and still have enough to export. That's an impressive fact for a country with limited water resources and a small percentage of land that is suitable for growing crops. But agriculture is a minor part of Israel's economy, providing only 3 percent of Israel's exports. Nevertheless, it's an important part and reflects the many advances Israel has made in a short time.

Israel has had two distinct economic periods: the first from 1948 to 1972, and the second from 1973 to the present. The beginning of the first period was extremely difficult. As a new state, Israel had a bare economic framework and limited natural resources and public services. In addition, Israel had to protect itself from neighboring countries—which were not receptive to the establishment of the State of Israel—and at the same time accommodate new immigrants.

Israel faced no small task. It had to provide its new arrivals with food, housing, and clothing, and set up civil service, monetary, and economic systems. Meanwhile, the neighboring Arab countries had blocked free trade with Israel.

ECONOMIC GROWTH

Israel overcame its early economic problems partly because of foreign investment and external aid. It received gifts, loans, and grants from the United States, donations from Jews around the world, and reparation funds from West Germany for crimes against Jews during World War II. That, combined with the resourcefulness of the Israelis, provided the great push for the country's economic growth. From the late 1940s until the mid-1970s, Israeli goods and services increased 10 percent annually, which was never matched by any other country in the free world for the same period.

The second economic period began in 1973. There were periods of strong growth followed by periods of stagnation and high unemployment. Nonetheless, in the 1970s, Israel had achieved a standard of living close to that of Western countries. The 1973 Yom Kippur War, however, created new economic woes. The United States continued to provide aid, however, which eased Israel's burden.

By 1990, Israel was producing goods and services worth $50 billion. Inflation—an economic condition in which prices rise rapidly—was rampant, however, and strict price controls were imposed on essential goods. Tariffs, a type of extra fee, were placed on imported goods, and a tax on travel was implemented. These efforts proved successful as inflation came down to a more manageable level.

A container ship from Turkey arrives at the Port of Haifa in Israel.

Today, due to its limited natural resources, Israel continues to rely on imports. It still imports far more than it exports, creating a large trade deficit—a generally unfavorable situation for an economy.

The government plays a significant role in Israel's economy; it owns and operates the postal, telegraph, and telephone systems as well as the railways. Public works, which includes the building of roads, bridges, and infrastructure, generates many jobs.

Much of Israel's national income comes from manufacturing, agriculture, communications, computer-aided design, and medical electronics.

THE LABOR FORCE AND UNIONS

Nearly all workers in Israel are members of a union. Although there are four labor unions, the most influential one is the *Histadrut*, or "General Federation of Labor." It was created in 1923 by the Zionist workers' movement. The Histadrut operates social service programs, develops industrial projects, and provides free education programs.

In 1989 the Histadrut had a membership of more than 1.5 million members. However, because of the privatization of the federation's

healthcare system and its link to mandatory Histadrut membership, the number of members has fallen to around 650,000. The Histadrut has no religious or ethnic criteria for its members. Arab and Druze workers are also full members. All types of workers make up the Histadrut: professional, technical, agricultural, civil service, and industrial.

The other three unions in Israel represent approximately 250,000 workers. Two of these, *Poale I Agudat Israel* (POH-ahl-leh ah-goo-DAHT ISS-rah-ell) and *Ha-Poel Ha-Mizrachi* (ah-poh-ELL ah-miz-rah-HEE), are religious unions that occasionally team up with the Histadrut on certain projects. Poale I Agudat Israel is a Jewish movement and political party that promotes adherence to religious law. It includes rabbinical, political, and executive branches and has a worldwide network of religious schools. The Ha-Poel Ha-Mizrachi combines the Torah, Zionism, and socialism into one movement. The fourth union is the National Labor Federation.

Thousands of Israeli union members demonstrate outside government buildings in Jerusalem to protest a new economic plan concerning their pensions.

AGRICULTURE

Early settlers created the kibbutzim (collective farms) to fulfill their dreams in the "land of milk and honey." After 1948, however, when Arab nations blocked trade with the new Israeli nation, it became an economic necessity to develop other sources to produce food that previously had been imported from Arab countries.

Although only 20 percent of Israel's land could be farmed, the imagination and skills of the people paved the way for success. Marshland was drained and rocks moved to reveal usable farmland. Where there was no water, irrigation systems and greenhouses were built. All these measures increased the amount of arable land. Today nearly all of Israel's food needs are met

by its agricultural production, and the country even produces enough food that some of it can be exported. With all of this efficiency, just 2 percent of Israel's labor force is engaged in agricultural activities.

MANUFACTURING

About 16 percent of Israel's workers are involved in manufacturing, and manufacturing generates 31.2 percent of the national income.

The greatest concentration of heavy industry is in the Haifa area, while Tel Aviv is home to light industries such as textile manufacturing and food processing. Shoes, pencils, and printed items are produced in Jerusalem.

The Dead Sea does not support life, but it supports the economy by providing valuable salt and minerals.

Another prospering sector is the diamond industry, although the gems are mined in other countries, such as Africa, Australia, Canada, and Russia. Diamond cutting, polishing, and trade originated in the town of Netanya in Israel. Today the center of these activities is Tel Aviv, where the Israel Diamond Exchange is among the world's largest diamond markets.

MINERAL WEALTH

The Dead Sea provides large quantities of potash and bromine, and contains generous salt deposits. The desert also yields valuable minerals: granite and phosphates in the Negev, and minerals for making glass and porcelain near Beersheba. Oil, too, is found in the Negev, in its northern area, as well as northeast of Beersheba.

FISHING

Fishing has developed into an important industry, with freshwater fish from the Sea of Galilee (also called the Kinneret) as well as the saltwater

FOOD FROM THE DESERT

In the early 1900s, when the Zionist movement was beginning, Jewish settlers came to their promised land and encountered a poverty-stricken countryside of sand dunes and swamps. Their first order of business was to prepare the land for settlement and fully utilize whatever natural resources they could find.

This remains a priority for Israel. Right in the middle of the Negev Desert, where the temperature can exceed 120°F (49°C) and there is an annual rainfall of less than an inch, agricultural settlements thrive. Israel has revolutionized its management of land and water resources in desert environments. What makes this feat so great is that the crops are not only irrigated using underground water, but also brackish salty water.

This is possible through the process of desalination to remove salt from salt water. However, because desalination was very costly, the developers of the Negev settlement cultivated plants that did not soak up salt. It took scientists six years of experimentation to strike a correct balance of water nutrients, salt, and sun. The process, known as brackish-water agriculture, has made great strides. It has perfected the Negev tomato, which is quite popular in Europe because of its rich taste and ability to stay fresh for about a month. In addition, brackish-water agriculture has enabled Israel to become a world leader in agricultural exports.

The amount of cotton produced in Israel now surpasses that produced in Egypt and in the states of California and Arizona. Peanut production in Israel is more than four times that of Georgia and West Virginia. Israelis hope that in a few years the Negev will be the main producer of winter vegetables for Europe.

offerings from the Mediterranean Sea. Israelis also send boats as far out as the Ethiopian coast and the Atlantic Ocean to fish, in order to find greater numbers and more varieties of fish species. About one-third of the fish netted by Israeli fishing boats are freshwater varieties raised in artificial ponds, many of which are part of a kibbutz fish farming operation.

TOURISM

Tourism is a vital source of income and foreign currency for Israel. In 2013, a record of 3.54 million tourists visited Israel, with the most popular site being the Western Wall in the Old City of Jerusalem with 68 percent of tourists visiting there. Israel has the highest number of museums per capita in the world. Israel's main tourist attractions are its historical sites and places of importance for three of the world's main religions. Devotees flock to the country during the seasons of Advent, Christmas, Ramadan, Hanukkah, Yom Kippur, Passover, Lent, and Easter. As Israel is a country of immigrants, most Israelis maintain ties with family members and friends from all over the world. These visiting relatives and friends form a sizeable portion of tourist arrivals in Israel.

However, Israel is also prone to civil violence and warfare, which break out frequently. Citizens, tourists, and religious pilgrims have been injured as a result of these incidents. The volatile political and religious climate prevailing over Israel in recent years has hurt the country's tourism industry.

INTERNET LINKS

www.financeisrael.mof.gov.il
State of Israel Ministry of Finance
An economic overview plus reports and links.

www.myjewishlearning.com/israel/Contemporary_Life/Society_and_Religious_Issues/Agriculture.shtml
My Jewish Learning
An article on agriculture in Israel on an excellent site with many different topics.

www.independent.co.uk/news/world/middle-east/an-insiders-guide-to-life-on-a-kibbutz-424166.html
The Independent: "An Insider's Guide to Life on a Kibbutz"
A fascinating, first-person narrative about a visit to a kibbutz.

ENVIRONMENT

An ostrich and her young live at Yotvada Hai-Bar Nature Reserves in the Negev Desert.

5

ISRAEL'S ENVIRONMENT IS A SOURCE OF pride, for environmental achievements made over the course of a short time. Israel's environment is a source of wonder due to the many majestic, scenic places found across the diverse natural terrain of this small country. Israel's environment is a source of conflict, though, as Jews and Palestinians battle over natural resources. Ultimately, Israel's environment is a source of identity, where the people find their ancient roots in the lands of the Bible.

Israelis see a call to environmental preservation in the Bible, which informs people of their rights and responsibilities as stewards of the Earth. For example, the book of Genesis calls on people to "...rule over the fish of the sea and the birds of the air and over every living creature that moves on the ground", while Deuteronomy instructs "...do not destroy [its] trees."

Teachings on preserving the land through conservation and development are found throughout Jewish law and literature. For instance, there is a command in the Bible to let the land rest every seventh year, which is practiced throughout Israel, and which has been cited as a means of soil preservation and improvement.

The Israelis have taken a dry land, which has a varied and difficult climate and a growing population, and made it blossom. The people of this historically arid land have become world leaders in agricultural innovation, pollution prevention and control, and waste management.

AIR POLLUTION

With increased urbanization and industrialization, Israel has developed programs to deal with air pollution, water shortages, and increasing amounts of solid and hazardous waste.

The main sources of air pollution in Israel are energy production, vehicular traffic, and industrial activities. Israel has worked to improve the air quality by establishing a nationwide framework for monitoring and analyzing air pollution, by implementing legislation, and by initiating research and development to examine alternative energy resources.

The national system that collects and analyzes data on air quality includes twenty-four sophisticated monitoring stations, three regional centers, and a

A bicycle-sharing service in Tel Aviv provides an alternative to driving.

national control center. This system monitors the air for pollutants such as ozone and sulfur dioxide. Israel is an international leader in the development and use of solar power and other alternative energy sources.

WATER CONSERVATION

Water shortage is a major environmental issue in Israel. This is due to the limited natural water resources and a rising demand for water from industry, agriculture, and a growing population.

To combat the water shortage, Israel has undertaken a multifaceted strategy that combines education, technical development, and financial incentives. Technological innovations have been pursued both to use water more efficiently and to treat and reuse waste water. Israel has been able to conserve water through the development of innovative irrigation methods and the introduction of crops that can live on limited water or on saltwater. The government has built water treatment plants in the major cities and recycles 70 percent of its waste water for irrigation of non-food crops and animal consumption.

THE POLITICS OF WATER

One of the Palestinian people's main complaints against Israel has to do with water. In short, Israel controls much of the water supply, and gets more of it than the Palestinians do. West Bank and Gaza Strip residents continuously suffer severe water shortages. Part of the problem is geographical, but much of it is political.

The country's main source of fresh water is the Jordan River basin, and specifically the Sea of Galilee in the north. Water in this dry land also comes from aquifers, which are underground sources, including the West Bank Mountain Aquifer and the Coastal Aquifer. In the 1967 Six-Day War, Israel gained exclusive control of the waters of the West Bank and the Sea of Galilee. Today Israel gets about 60 percent of its water from those resources.

The underground resources are shared by the Israelis and the Palestinians, and Nature knows no political boundaries. However, the division of that groundwater is subject to the provisions of the Oslo Accords of 1995—a plan that was meant to be in place for only five years, pending further peace talks, which never materialized. For example, the Oslo agreement gives 80 percent of the Mountain Aquifer water to Israel, and 20 percent to the Palestinians of the West Bank. In addition, the agreement stipulates no cap to the supply of water to Israelis, whereas the water supply to Palestinians is limited to predetermined amounts. The only water available to the people in the Gaza Strip is that of the Coastal Aquifer, which is being drawn down at too rapid a rate, allowing saltwater to seep in. Drinking water in Gaza is therefore brackish, poor quality water.

The situation, like so many affecting the Israelis and Palestinians, is complex. Israelis point to their own initiatives in desalinating and recycling water to meet their own needs. Palestinians answer that they cannot afford to undertake such projects, especially with the blockade of the Gaza Strip, and that at any rate, the Israelis are preventing them from accessing their own water. Presently, the Palestinians have insufficient water and must purchase extra from Mekorot, Israel's national water company.

WASTE MANAGEMENT

Waste disposal in Israel was largely unregulated until 1993, when the government began developing central sanitary landfills and closing illegal dumpsites.

A crane removes garbage from a dumpster at a recycling center.

Israel generates 6 million tons (5.4 million tonnes) of solid waste annually, and the government is working on plants that convert this waste to useful energy. Israelis, who produce an average of 1,300 pounds (590 kg) of waste per year, are also encouraged to reduce waste by recycling more goods.

Israel manages hazardous substances with numerous strictly enforced laws and regulations. It has a national response system that can send inspectors to the scene of a hazardous substance accident within a half hour, and a center for hazardous waste treatment and disposal.

NATURE CONSERVATION

Aware of its relatively small size and limited natural resources, Israel has taken steps to conserve whatever flora and fauna it has.

About 25 percent of Israel's land is protected. The country has 155 nature reserves, which include the wide range of Israel's various landscapes from forests to deserts. In addition, several of Israel's plants and animals (such as the leopard, gazelle, ibex, and vulture) have been given protected status. To preserve the natural landscapes, Israel has established forty-one national parks and implemented a national strategy for the development and conservation of forests.

A joint project of the Yotvada Hai-Bar Nature Reserves in the southern Arabah (desert environment) and the Carmel Hai-Bar Nature Reserve in the Carmel Mountains of northwestern Israel (Mediterranean forest environment) involves reintroducing animal species that once roamed Israel

A mountain goat
roams the Ein Gedi
Nature Reserve
west of the
Dead Sea.

into their former natural habitats. These species include the white oryx, ostrich, Persian fallow deer, roe deer, and Asiatic wild ass.

Wildflowers, which used to grow in abundance in Israel, had almost disappeared due to over picking in the 1960s. A successful government campaign managed to repair this damage. Today, Israelis are careful to avoid picking wildflowers, which once again bloom in profusion throughout the country.

ENVIRONMENTAL LEGISLATION

Over the last twenty years, Israel has worked to develop comprehensive environmental legislation. There are approximately twenty-four laws, which have criminal sanctions in the form of fines and imprisonment, and fifty-six regulations that deal with environmental issues.

Israel emphasizes strict enforcement of its environmental legislation through licensing and supervision as well as inspection and prosecution. Industries and businesses must fulfill certain conditions before they are licensed to operate. Parties who break the rules may have their businesses closed down.

Enforcement is done by the government through an investigating unit called The Environmental Patrol and through recruitment of volunteer civilians as Cleanliness Trustees who assist in the enforcement of the Maintenance of Cleanliness Law. This law ensures general cleanliness and order in Israel and prohibits such acts as littering and the improper disposal of waste, building debris, or vehicle scrap.

INTERNET LINKS

www.foeme.org
Friends of the Earth Middle East (FoEME)
An organization of cooperative Jordanian, Israeli, and Palestinian environmentalists.

www.sviva.gov.il/English/Pages/HomePage.aspx
Israel Ministry of Environmental Protection
Environmental news and information, some in Hebrew only.

www.jewishvirtuallibrary.org/jsource/Environment/envttoc.html
Jewish Virtual Library, Israel: Environment and Nature
Information about plants, animals, national parks, conservation, legislation, and more.

www.nytimes.com/2014/02/09/opinion/sunday/friedman-whose-garbage-is-this-anyway.html
New York Times, Thomas L. Friedman, "Whose Garbage Is This Anyway?"
A hard-hitting look at the environmental crises facing Israel and the Palestinians.

parks.org.il
Israel Nature and Parks Authority, select English
A guide to Israel's national parks, including World Heritage sites and Holy Land sites.

Two Israelis dance on Rothschild Boulevard in Tel Aviv.

6

IF ISRAEL IS THE DREAM, THEN THE Israelis are the dreamers. Certainly the early Zionist pioneers who saw a desert and imagined a garden were dreamers. Surely the waves of desperate people who fled the European nightmare of death for a new life were dreamers. And today, the citizens of one of the most controversial and conflicted nations on Earth, who stubbornly defend their existence—truly they are dreamers. For they still cling to the most elusive dream of all, peace.

● ● ● ● ● ● ● ● ● ● ● ● ●

"In Israel, in order to be a realist you must believe in miracles."
–David Ben-Gurion, first prime minister of Israel, in an interview on CBS in 1956

Yet there's nothing soft and fluffy about these people. Israelis are made of tough stuff. These are people who are often accused of being rude, hard edged, and barbed—and they know it. There's a reason native-born Israelis are called *Sabras*; these "prickly pears" are thorny on the outside. They have to be able to survive in a dangerous environment, after all.

Naturally, all people are not the same and broad generalizations risk turning into stereotypes. Israelis are made up of very different kinds of people, and some who are not Jewish at all.

The estimated population of Israel is six million. Of that figure, around 75 percent are Jewish and 25 percent are non-Jewish citizens, most of whom are Arab.

Ethiopian Jews arrive in Israel during Operation Soloman in 1991.

World events have had an impact on the population statistics of Israel: the breakup of the Soviet Union resulted in more than 340,000 Jewish immigrants added to Israel's population between mid-1989 and the end of 1991; famine in Ethiopia in the mid-1980s resulted in an airlift of 10,000 Ethiopian Jews to Israel; and in the spring of 1991, Operation Solomon, an airlift of 14,500 additional Ethiopians, was carried out just before the Ethiopian government fell to rebel forces.

The Law of Return, which grants citizenship to any Jew who migrates to Israel, ensures that there will always be a place for Jews in Israel. (This does not apply to Palestinians who want to return to land they consider their own, having been displaced in 1948 at the creation of Israel. That, of course, is another source of conflict.)

JEWISH ETHNIC GROUPS

The Diaspora—the dispersion of Jews dating back to the second century—was the most significant influence on the creation of different ethnic groups within Judaism. These people were scattered throughout the world and lacked a homeland. Although they clung to the study and observance of Jewish religious scriptures and attempted to follow the laws and rituals of the religion, they adopted many new attitudes in the foreign lands where they came to reside.

Indeed the Jews of Israel share a common identity through Judaism, but they are not an identical people. Coming back to the Holy Land from more than 100 countries, they bring numerous languages and customs.

There are two dominant Jewish ethnic groups in Israel—the Ashkenazim and the Sephardim. The Ashkenazim, whose name comes from the old

Hebrew word for Germany, are Jews from northern and eastern Europe and Russia. The Hebrew word *Sephard* means a Jewish person from Spain. In the fifteenth century, Jews who refused to convert to Christianity were forced to leave Spain and Portugal. Many fled to North Africa, Italy, and what is now Turkey. Today, Sephardic refers to Jews from Aegean, Mediterranean, Balkan, and Middle Eastern backgrounds.

The Ashkenazim were among the leaders of the Zionist movement who brought with them the Western lifestyles that set the pace for Israel's cultural and intellectual development. The Sephardim, on the other hand, made up the majority of immigrants after 1950. Many were from small villages in North Africa, Iraq, Syria, Greece, and Turkey.

Another major difference between these two groups was their view of Israel. The Sephardim saw life in Israel as delivery from exile and the fulfillment of a biblical prophecy. The Ashkenazim had suffered persecution in their former homelands and hoped to find political and religious freedom in the Jewish state.

IMMIGRATION TRENDS

The word *aliyah*, which literally means "going up," refers to the immigration of Jews to the land of Israel. Five major periods of aliyah have contributed to the development of Israel's people.

The First Aliyah, from 1882 to 1903, brought 25,000 Jews—mostly fleeing persecution in Russia. Their arrival was partly influenced by *Hibbat Tzion*, or "Love of Zion," a movement for the reestablishment of Israel, which started among the Jews in Russia and spread to other countries at the end of the nineteenth century. Their arrival in Palestine doubled the Jewish population and caused the first clash between the Ashkenazim and the Sephardim. These immigrants were less religious and more interested in establishing a Jewish nation, while the Palestinian Jews were not as political and more religious. Several thousand Jews from Yemen also arrived with the First Aliyah.

The First Aliyah immigrants were responsible for starting early rural settlements. It was also during this time that Hebrew was first revived as a means of communication, aided by the setting up of Hebrew schools.

The Second and Third Aliyot (*aliyot* is the plural of aliyah), from 1904 to 1923, brought 76,000 Jews mainly from Russia and Poland. These aliyot were encouraged by the Balfour Declaration of 1917 and the British occupation of Palestine, which later spurred the creation of the Jewish state of Israel. Immigrants of the Second and Third Aliyot created kibbutzim, cooperative villages called *moshavim*, and the Histadrut labor federation. They also fortified the education system. They used Hebrew in all areas of Jewish life and laid the foundation for modern Tel Aviv.

Approximately 349,000 central European immigrants came in the Fourth and Fifth Aliyot, from 1924 to 1939. Many of them fled their homes to escape Nazism, which began when Adolf Hitler came to power and set out to exterminate all the Jews in Europe. Immigrants of the Fourth and Fifth Aliyot, many of whom were professionals and businessmen, contributed greatly to the cultural and economic development of the country. These immigrants settled in the major cities and towns; half of them chose Tel Aviv, where they were able to continue a way of life that was similar to what they had grown accustomed to in Europe.

Immigrants from 1948 to 1969 numbered 1.25 million; half were from Asia and North Africa. Compared to the Askenazim, the Sephardim were socially and economically disadvantaged from the start of their stay in Israel. The Sephardim Jews lacked skills and education and had to accept lower paying jobs. They also often had larger families and lived in marginal neighborhoods, and this hampered their social mobility.

While in theory the Sephardim Jews were accepted into Israeli society, the rift between them and the Askenazim gained a strong foothold and problems of discrimination and inequality persist.

ISRAELI ARABS

The Israeli Arab population, more than three-quarters of whom are Sunni Muslims, has remained concentrated in the northern and Haifa districts since 1948. Israel's establishment in 1948 also absorbed one million Palestinians, who stayed on and became part of Israel.

A poor Arab village lies outside the Old City of Jerusalem.

A Bedouin man grinds coffee in his tent in the Negev Desert.

Approximately two-thirds of Israel's Arab citizenry live in urban areas and are mainly employed in construction and industry rather than agricultural occupations. Arabs, mostly Muslims, make up 20 percent of Israel's population, making them an ethnic and religious minority.

As citizens, the Arabs share in the health, welfare, and education systems. Arab citizens have voting rights and government representation. They are exempted from military service, but they have less access to land ownership and certain types of government funding. Arab sympathy for the Palestine Liberation Organization makes for resentment and ill feelings between the Jewish majority and the Arab minority.

Israeli Arabs generally remain loyal to their cultural, religious, and political backgrounds. Like the Jews, even though they share a common ethnic identity, the Arabs are made up of different groups of people.

THE BEDOUINS

The Bedouin population in Israel represents some forty Arab tribal groups living primarily in the Negev Desert in southern Israel. Traditionally they were nomads; however some are now settled in small villages and towns. Bedouins are found in many countries in the Middle East, about 200,000 live in Israel.

Nomadic Bedouins eat, sleep, travel, and trade in much the same way that they did 1,500 years ago. Along with their camels, they are well known for having conquered the desert. They live mostly by herding camel, goat, and sheep, and are considered good traders. They are also great hosts; whenever they have visitors, they always give their very best food. The Bedouins pride themselves on their hospitality, which they treat their guests to, along with protection. A guest who dines in a Bedouin home has protection for as long as three days after the meal.

Bedouin nomads are said to have an uncanny tracking ability; they are known as the best desert trackers in the world. They are able to find traces of people or animals in the sand, tell if the animal had been running, or whether a man or woman was carrying equipment.

This skill has made Bedouins very valuable to the Israeli army, especially for guarding the borders. They are among the few Israeli Arabs who can serve in the army, and may be called upon to track down enemy troops who have broken through Israel's border defenses.

THE DRUZE

The Druze, also called the Muwahideen, are an Arab sect that established its own branch of Islam in the eleventh century. One of the most fascinating things about this group is that they have kept their religion a secret. They do not accept converts, leave their faith, or marry other than their fellow Druze. This exclusive sect lives by its own principles and prefers to remain closed to public scrutiny.

A Druze man picks apples in the Golan Heights.

The Druze live in the area where Syria, Lebanon, and Israel meet. They number around 120,000 in Israel, many living in the Golan Heights, and make their living by farming. The Israeli Druze have adapted to Israeli society better than any other Arab group and, unlike most Arabs, are pro-Israel. For years, the Druze have served in the army, and they have representatives in the Knesset. In recent years, however, some younger Druze are refusing to serve, claiming conscientious objector status instead.

The one exception to the generally friendly Jewish-Druze relationship involves the Druze of the Golan Heights. Although these Arabs have been Israeli citizens since the 1967 war, they feel they are unwilling victims of the Israeli-Syrian dispute, and so they choose not to vote and do not go into the army. Unlike other Arabs in the Gaza Strip and the West Bank, however, they do not openly oppose Israel.

A recent wave of Sephardic immigrants, the Ethiopian Jews, have quite different religious customs from the other Jewish groups that have returned to the Holy Land—so different that their "Jewishness" was a topic of conversation among Israel's chief rabbis. The differences are the result of the Ethiopians' isolation from mainstream Judaism.

What caused that isolation? According to Jewish history, twelve ancient tribes lived in Palestine. After years of fighting among themselves, the land was divided into the kingdom of Israel in the north, where ten tribes lived, and the kingdom of Judah in the south, home to the remaining two tribes.

In 722 BCE the kingdom of Israel was conquered by the Assyrians, and its inhabitants exiled to "Halah and Habor by the river Gozan, and in the cities of Medes." These ten tribes were never seen again, and they are known as the Ten Lost Tribes of Israel.

Biblical prophets Isaiah, Jeremiah, and Ezekiel promised that the lost tribes would eventually be reunited with the rest of the nation, and this has kept the memory and search for the tribes alive. Thus many think that the return of the Ethiopian Jews to Israel is a 10 percent fulfillment of that prophecy.

Throughout history, attempts have been made to explain how the ten tribes disappeared and to discover what became of them. An 1871 book even presented forty-seven supposed proofs that the British were part of the Ten Lost Tribes.

The search goes on. For the last three decades, an organization called Amishav has been dedicated to finding lost Jews from around the world. The group's mission is to return these people to the land, for according to biblical prophecy, the Messiah will come only after all twelve tribes return to Israel.

However, there are skeptics who dismiss the Ten Lost Tribes as nothing but legend, as there is no conclusive evidence to prove their existence.

OTHER MINORITIES

There are also small communities of Karaites (30,000) who adhere to the Torah but not the Talmudic texts, in the towns of Ashdod, Beersheba, and Ramla; Circassians (4,000), a band of relocated Islamic converts from the Caucasus Mountains in two villages in Galilee; and Samaritans (750) in the towns of Holon and Shechem.

A mosque in the Muslim quarter of Nazareth in Galilee.

INTERNET LINKS

www.ifcj.org/site/PageNavigator/sfi_about_culture_ethnicities
Stand for Israel: the Holy Land Today—Ethnic Groups
Articles about eight of the largest ethnic groups in Israel.

electronicintifada.net
The Electronic Intifada
An independent online news publication from the Arab resistance point of view: covering Palestinian politics and culture.

news.bbc.co.uk/2/hi/middle_east/8165338.stm
BBC News: Q&A: Israeli Arabs
A frank, quick discussion of the status of Israeli Arabs.

www.bbc.com/travel/feature/20130820-israels-forgotten-tribe/1
BBC Travel: Israel's Forgotten Tribe
A look at the Druze and their place in Israel.

www.pbs.org/wgbh/nova/israel
PBS, Nova: "Lost Tribes of Israel"
The fascinating companion website to a Nova program from 2000.

LIFESTYLE

Young Israelis sit outside at a café in Nahalat Shiva, a neighborhood in central Jerusalem.

7

LIFE IN ISRAEL IS VERY MUCH LIKE LIFE in any other advanced, industrialized country. People go to work, children go to school, most people follow the rules, and most people get along just fine. Every day brings its blessings and problems, small and large—the sound of children singing, the fragrance of bread baking, the traffic jams, or the latest catastrophe in the news. Life goes on just like it does everywhere.

Bike riders traverse the famous Beeri cycling route in Israel.

The Israel National Trail is a hiking path that crosses the entire country. Its northern end is at Dan near the borders of Syria and Lebanon, and it extends to Eilat at the southernmost tip of Israel on the Red Sea. The trail is about 580 miles (940 km) long and takes about thirty to seventy days of hiking to complete.

The difference is that, for most Israelis, their lifestyle is uniquely Jewish. Of course, many Jews live in other countries and may live a very Jewish lifestyle indeed, but in no other country are Jews the majority culture. And that makes all the difference.

A fundamental principle of the state of Israel is that every Jew has the right to settle there. The Law of Return gives legal status to this principle; it grants automatic citizenship to any Jew who wants it. Also guaranteed is freedom of worship. As a result of this, there are many lifestyles within this tiny nation. Israeli society is a kaleidoscope of customs, traditions, and beliefs. The ways in which these groups conduct their lives and interact with one another—or perhaps don't—present a very interesting picture.

JUDAISM IN EVERYDAY LIFE

Judaism is the unifying force and basis for the establishment of the state of Israel. The bond among the Jewish sects strengthens during times of Arab opposition. Nonetheless, deep divisions exist in the Israeli Jewish communities and continue to be important.

The major difference among Israelis is between religious Jews and secular Jews, and over the separation of synagogue and government. More than 75 percent of Israel's Jews consider themselves secular. Of those, some may be religious in their personal lives and others may not be, but either way, they do not want religion dictating the policies of government. The other 25 percent wants to see the country run according to religious laws. While it would seem that the religious minority would not play a significant role in Israeli day-to-day life, quite the opposite is true. Religious groups form political parties, and even a small group can exert considerable political influence.

Religious Jews feel that because Israel is a Jewish state, it should be based on Jewish customs and laws, and that the secular part affecting Jewish life should be checked. They maintain that Jewish tradition is what held the Jewish people together during centuries of separation, and it is what led to the establishment of Israel.

On the other hand, secular Israelis insist that religious involvement should be a matter of personal choice and that in a democracy, separation

The most devout religious people in Israel are the ultra-Orthodox Jews. They make up about 11.5 percent of the country's population. They are called ultra-Orthodox because of their rejection of secular society and their strict adherence to Jewish law in all parts of their life. However, these Jews find the name to be derogatory because they think it implies extremism. They don't consider their lifestyle to be extreme, but merely correct. They call themselves Haredi Jews or Haredim.

Communities of Haredim, including Hasidic Jews and other sects, are also found in Europe and North America. Wherever they live, they tend to isolate themselves from the rest of society, at least as much as possible. Their lives are directed by rigid laws that govern how they will dress, eat, and behave. Dress is conservative, with men wearing black suits with long overcoats and black brimmed hats. They usually have beards and sidelocks. Women dress modestly with high necklines, long skirts, and long sleeves. They never wear slacks. Married women must cover their hair.

About 60 percent of Haredi men in Israel are not employed, but rather study the Torah as their full-time vocation. They live on government subsidies, charitable gifts, and, sometimes, their wives' wages. Women may work as teachers in girls' schools and in a limited number of other occupations. In addition, these people typically have large families with many children.

Until recently, the Haredi were exempt from service in Israel's military. However, that law didn't sit well with many of Israel's other citizens, who considered it unfair. The Haredi claim that military service would expose them to secular culture, which is forbidden. Many are not Zionists and believe the Jews should have waited for the coming of the Messiah before establishing a homeland, and therefore don't share the passion for defending the country that other Israelis often have. In March 2014, however, Israel's parliament approved legislation to end exemptions from military service for Haredi religious students. This ultra-Orthodox community decried the move as a "war against religion."

of religion and government is key. And because Judaism is considered to be not just a religion but, rather, a way of life, secular Jews believe that the imposition of religious ritual and tradition prevents them from enjoying the religious freedom that is guaranteed in Israel.

EDUCATION

Israeli law states that for Jews, primary education should focus on "the values of Jewish culture and the achievements of science; on love of the homeland and devotion to the state and the Jewish people; on training in agricultural work and handicraft; on fulfillment of pioneering principles; and on the aspiration to a society built on freedom, equality, tolerance, mutual assistance, and love of mankind."

Students congregate on the lawn at Ben Gurion University of the Negev in Be'er Sheva, Israel.

Free education is a cornerstone of democracy in the state of Israel, and it is a prime national concern. In Israel, education is compulsory and free for children (Jews, Arabs, and other ethnic minorities alike) between the ages of five and sixteen. The system includes kindergarten, six-year primary schools, three-year junior high schools, and three-year high schools. After high school, students take an exam to determine if they can go on to college. University education is usually pursued after military service.

The government runs three types of schools: secular (without religious connections), religious (which devote attention to religious laws, prayers, and the Talmud, a supreme sourcebook of law), and schools for Israeli Arabs. Private religious schools, run by independent orthodox organizations, are also available. In religious institutions, boys and girls are educated in separate classes. After graduating from these schools at the age of fourteen, boys generally enter a *yeshiva* (yeh-SHI-vah), or religious college, to become rabbis. A rabbi is the main religious leader of a synagogue and its congregation.

Students attend school six days a week. In primary school, they study Hebrew, the Old Testament, geography, science, mathematics, crafts, art and music, history, and physical education. English classes start in the fifth grade, and Arabic is often taught as a third language.

Children from Arab villages and Bedouin camps can go to school too. For the Bedouins, there are field schools that move with the population. Arabic is the language of instruction in all Israeli Arab schools, and Hebrew is taught as a second language. Most teachers in these schools are Arabs, and emphasis is placed on Arabic history and culture. Textbooks used are direct Arabic translations of the Hebrew texts used in Jewish schools. In the Gaza Strip and the West Bank, schools are under the authority of the local municipality.

Post-secondary education is open to anyone who is qualified. There are twelve institutes of higher education in Israel. Hebrew University in Jerusalem and Tel Aviv University educate approximately 53,000 students between them. Others include the Ben Gurion University, Haifa University, and Bar Ilan University. The Technion in Haifa and the Weizmann Institute in Rehovot are well-known technology and science schools.

Israeli soldiers hold an urban warfare exercise at a military training base near the Tze'elim kibbutz in the Negev Desert.

THE ARMY

The Israeli army (also known as the Israel Defense Forces, or IDF) plays an important part in the lives of all young Jewish Israelis. The average Sabra

A student from New York is learning Hebrew in an ulpan class.

grows up knowing that once he or she reaches the age of seventeen or eighteen, military service is next.

All Jewish citizens must serve, except those who are handicapped. Although military service is compulsory, Israelis look upon it with pride and joy. Men serve for three years, women for two. In addition, men must serve four weeks in the active reserves each year until they reach the age of fifty-one. Unmarried women remain in the reserves until they are thirty-four.

The military also serves a social function in Israel. Because Jews who immigrate to Israel are granted immediate citizenship, the new arrival's first duty is military service. While in the army, he or she learns to speak and read Hebrew, studies the history and geography of the new country, and is taught everything about Israeli citizenship.

While in the army, many get a head start on a career by seeking army jobs in fields that they would like to enter later on. Becoming an officer is also beneficial; the most successful executives, managers, and government employees were officers during their military service, so the youth generally take their time in the IDF very seriously.

ULPAN

The *ulpan* (ool-PAHN) is a special school that teaches immigrants about the cultures of Israel and offers intensive Hebrew language lessons. These lessons help immigrants to better assimilate into their new environment. New immigrants may also receive the absorption basket, which is a form of financial aid.

There are several types of ulpan: for example, the residential ulpan is

popular among professionals and meets for five hours a day for five months; the kibbutz for younger people has students working for four hours and studying the rest of the day.

Israeli Scouts get ready to leave for an autumn trip in the city of Kfar Saba.

YOUTH MOVEMENTS

Israeli youth organizations are active as extracurricular education and recreation for children and teenagers between the ages of ten and sixteen. Almost every young Israeli is a member of a youth movement. The largest group has ties with the Histadrut labor organization, serving as a type of junior trade union that provides vocational education and union benefits.

The Israel Scout Federation meets weekly for games, cultural activities, and educational programs. Members wear khaki uniforms and colorful kerchiefs, and leaders stress the importance of the pioneering spirit and the benefits of living off the land. This group is associated with the International Scouting Movement. Bene Akiva is the largest religious youth movement.

LIFE ON A KIBBUTZ

In the early 1900s, Jewish immigrants from Eastern Europe began buying plots of land in Israel and setting up farming communities called kibbutzim *(singular is* kibbutz*). These people lived and worked together according to idealistic, socialist values. Although the work was often very difficult, the Zionist pioneering spirit fueled their efforts. Everyone worked for the good of the kibbutz rather than for themselves. There were no owners, no employees, and no private property; all of the land, buildings, and tools belonged to the group. Food, shelter, clothing, health care, and education were provided.*

Most of the first kibbutzim were agricultural in nature, but over the years, some have turned to other sorts of industries as a means of earning money. Some collectives are secular while others are religious. All are based on democratic values of equality. The kibbutz provides for all the needs of its residents, and no one is paid for his or her work. Many kibbutznik, *or residents, eat in communal dining rooms, get their clothing from the community's shop, and have it washed at a communal laundry.*

Committees are elected to deal with management issues. Decisions are made at weekly meetings, and everything that is produced and earned is shared equally with all members.

Over the years, kibbutz culture has adapted to changing times. In the early days, for example, the community took precedence over the family. Children were raised together rather than with their families. Today the emphasis has shifted to the family unit, however, and most children live with their parents until they enter high school. All kibbutz youngsters, however, have their own jobs and often have to take care of crops. They attend kibbutz schools, where the schedule includes time to work on the farm.

Today there are some 270 kibbutzim in Israel. They vary in size from eighty to more than 2,000 members. With a total of around 100,000 members, they represent about 2.5 percent of Israel's population. Many also bring in short-term workers, such as students from other countries who come to Israel for the experience.

THE FAMILY

The family has always been important in Jewish life. Although many different ethnic groups, lifestyles, and attitudes make up the Israeli population, one thing that remains the same is the importance of the close-knit family unit.

For most Israeli families, regardless of whether they are secular or religious, kibbutznik or city-dweller, dinner time is usually the focal point of the family experience, for it is often the only time other than on the sabbath that the entire family can be together.

Because of the religious atmosphere in Israel, most families celebrate the Jewish festivals as holidays, and they cherish this time as quality time with the family.

MARRIAGE

In Judaism, marriage is considered the ideal state of existence; it is the basic social institution that God established at the time of creation. The traditional marriage ceremony consists of two acts: *kiddushin* (ki-DOO-shin) and *nisuin* (ni-SOO-in). Kiddushin is the legal receiving of the bride by the groom. The groom hands over an object of value—usually a ring— to the bride in the presence of two witnesses and says, "Behold, you are consecrated unto me with this ring, according to the law of Moses and Israel." By this act, he states his intention to reserve the bride for himself. By accepting the item of value, the bride indicates that she agrees.

In the nisuin ceremony, the mothers of the bride and groom lead the bride to the *huppah* (koo-PAH), or bridal canopy, which symbolizes the groom's house, and the mothers give the bride their blessings. The groom is accompanied to the huppah by the fathers of the bride and groom. The ceremony is customarily performed in the presence of a *minyan* (MIN-yahn), a group of ten men. After the bride and groom drink from a goblet of wine, the groom places the wedding ring on the index finger of the bride's right hand and repeats what he said during the kiddushin. Seven marriage blessings are recited over another goblet of wine by several different people, and the groom concludes the ceremony by crushing a glass under his right foot. (The

BAR MITZVAH

At age thirteen Jewish males celebrate their bar mitzvah, which literally means "son of commandment" (bat mitzvah or "daughter of commandment" for girls). It is from this point on that Jewish youths are obligated by religious duties, such as fasting on Yom Kippur, among other things. They also have the right to participate in religious services, and be counted as one of the ten people, or minyan, whose presence are needed to form a congregation for communal prayer and to perform parts of certain religious services.

A child attends religious school for several years before bar mitzvah or bat mitzvah to learn about Jewish holidays, language, customs, and history. He will also learn how to read the Torah and recite the attendant prayers.

The bar mitzvah happens automatically without the need for a ceremony to mark it. Nevertheless, bar mitzvah ceremonies, which were introduced in the last century, have become more and more popular. Not only do they mark the stage when a child becomes an adult in the eyes of the Jewish community, the bar mitzvah ceremonies also provide an opportunity for extended family members to come together and celebrate.

During the ceremony, the young person who is the bar mitzvah or bat mitzvah chants blessings, recites the haftarah, which is a section of Jewish scripture containing the writings of the prophets, and reads the Torah portion of the week. A special meal is served during this occasion, which may take place in synagogues or at sites of historical or religious significance in Israel, such as the Western Wall, Southern Wall, or Masada.

For most Jews, this coming of age is an important and memorable part of their lives.

breaking of glass signifies a number of things, primarily the mourning of the destruction of the temple in Jerusalem in 70 CE. It may also remind the couple that the life they face together will have sorrow as well as joy.) After the ceremony, the couple may be led to a private room in which they spend time together. It is only after this private time that they are considered to be truly husband and wife.

A Haredi Jewish bride and groom sit during their wedding in the Mea Shearim neighborhood of Jerusalem in 2014.

DIVORCE

In Judaism, when a married couple no longer shares a loving relationship, it is acceptable to get a divorce. Marriage and divorce are seen as acts of free will. Divorce, nevertheless, saddens and deeply hurts all who are involved.

In Israel, Jewish divorce cases go through the Jewish Rabbinical Court. The *get* (geht) is the bill of divorce, the document releasing the woman from her marriage. The get itself is written on heavy white paper. Special ink that cannot be erased is used to write the text so that no changes can be made after it is written.

According to Jewish law, only after the get is delivered into the hands of the wife does the divorce take place. At the ceremony, the husband and wife meet before the *beth din* (beht-DIN), or Rabbinical Court, and the husband hands the wife the twelve-line get. Until she holds the document, the divorce is not finalized. After receiving the piece of paper, the wife either takes a few symbolic steps or walks into another room. At that point, she is considered once again an unmarried woman.

BIRTH RITUALS

Historically and culturally, there is greater joy at the birth of a boy than of a girl. Jewish birth rituals differ for boys and girls.

Jewish boys are initiated into Judaism on the eighth day of life, the day of the *brit milah*, or ritual circumcision. The brit (or bris) is a symbol of a

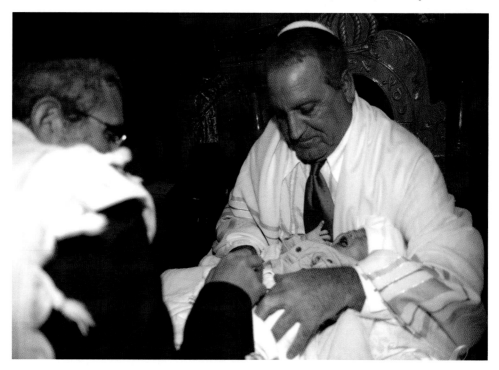

A Jewish infant boy receives a ritual circumcision at a ceremony in Jerusalem.

boy's joining the community of Israel. A *mohel* (maw-HELL), who is a ritual circumciser, performs the ceremony, which generally takes place at home in the presence of at least ten people. A pair of godparents is officially involved in the brit; the godfather (usually one of the grandfathers), who holds the baby, is designated the *sandak* (sahn-DAHK) and the godmother, who hands the baby to him is the *sandakit* (sahn-DAH-kit). Relatives and friends attend the brit, and a celebration takes place immediately after the ceremony.

There are no initiation rites for girls, although some modern Jews feel strongly that there should also be rites for Jewish girls. The father announces the name that has been chosen for his daughter in the synagogue in a blessing ceremony. This is usually done on the sabbath after the child's birth. In some synagogues, the baby's name may be inscribed on a parchment to mark the occasion of her naming.

INTERNET LINKS

www.jpost.com/LifeStyle/Home.aspx
Jerusalem Post Lifestyle section.

www.jerusalemonline.com/culture-and-lifestyle
Jerusalem Online Culture and Lifestyle section.

www.haaretz.com/opinion/.premium-1.583141
Haaretz
Israel's secular vs. ultra-Orthodox Jews: One people, divided?

time.com/21237/israel-ultra-orthodox-knesset-draft
Time, "Israel Passes Law Drafting Ultra-Orthodox Into the Army"
This article explains the recent ruling in Israel.

RELIGION

8

RELIGION IS ESSENTIAL TO ISRAEL.

Though individual Israelis may not be religious—some are not—and the country's government is secular, religion is built into Israel's identity.

It all starts in Genesis. Genesis is the first book of the Bible; the very word *genesis* means "beginning." Indeed, the book's first words are "In the beginning..." Genesis starts with the creation story—how God created the cosmos, Earth, life on Earth, and finally, Adam and Eve, the first man and woman. Genesis also explains the beginnings of Judaism—how God led Abraham to the land of Canaan, and promised it to all of his children. The children of Abraham became the first Jews, and the land of Canaan, the "Promised Land," became Israel.

When Israel was established as a Jewish nation in 1948, its founders could have chosen to make Judaism the exclusive state religion and ban all others. Other countries in the Middle East, such as Saudi Arabia, have done exactly that with Islam. But Israel's founders wanted a free country.

The Israeli Declaration of Independence guarantees freedom of worship and the safety of the holy places of all religions. Jerusalem is profoundly significant to not only Judaism, but also to Christianity and Islam, therefore different religious traditions are observed in Israel today.

Judaism is the majority religion in Israel. The religion forms the basic values on which the political structure of the government and Israel's nationhood are based.

"And I will give to you, and to your offspring after you, the land where you are now an alien, all the land of Canaan, for a perpetual holding; and I will be their God."
(Genesis 17:8)
–God speaking to Abraham, as related in the Bible

JUDAISM

"Hear, O Israel, the Lord our God, the Lord is One." This prayer is the fundamental message of Judaism. It refers to the covenant, or sacred agreement, that Jews will worship only one God and obey his laws. There is no priestly class between God and humanity, so Jews can appeal to God for help and praise him directly.

In Judaism, it is a person's relationship with God that is stressed. The rabbi is the person in the community who is responsible for religious education, guidance, and services in the synagogue. His or her position does not involve special privileges. Rabbis interpret Jewish law and guide the spiritual lives of the people.

In the covenant, contained in the first five books of the Bible, known as the Torah, God chose the descendants of Abraham to bring knowledge and acceptance of God to the world. Through this acceptance, the Torah says, all of humanity can have a place in heaven.

The Talmud, another collection of authoritative ancient writings, combines with the Torah to form the religious laws that govern the lives of the Jewish people. These laws include ideas about the equality and rights of all people, personal morality, and personal freedom.

Judaism focuses on the works of God throughout the past, present, and future. The focus on the past is through the study of the Jewish holy scripture; the present through living according to Jewish laws; and the future in anticipation of the coming Messiah.

Jewish laws are primarily concerned with moral values, teaching that people must be fair and kind to others, and that they should live a good life for the sake of being a good human being. The primary goal of Jewish law is to fulfill God's commandments.

THE SYNAGOGUE

The Jewish house of worship is the synagogue or temple. It is considered the house of God and his people, or a place of assembly for people in the presence of their God.

BRANCHES OF JUDAISM

Until the nineteenth century, there was only one approach to Jewish religious tradition. Judaism was practiced in the way that is called Orthodox Judaism. Today, there are three other main branches of the religion—Reform, Conservative, and Reconstructionist Judaism.

Orthodox means "the right way." People who adhere to this form of Judaism fully accept God's word as it was revealed to Moses in the Torah. Orthodox Jews strictly adhere to the Talmud and the later laws of the rabbis.

Strict observance of the Sabbath, kashrut (KAHSH-root), or dietary law, and holy days are characteristics of Orthodox Judaism. Synagogue services are conducted exclusively in Hebrew. Married women wear head coverings at all times as evidence of modesty. Men and women are separated during worship in an Orthodox synagogue.

Reform Judaism rejects many of the practices and beliefs of Orthodox Judaism, including the authority of the Talmud and dietary laws. The Reform movement began in Germany in the early 1800s when some Jews felt that they needed to lead their lives in a way that was closer to the lifestyles of the non-Jewish people around them.

In Reform Judaism, head coverings are optional, and women and men worship together. Women can even become rabbis. The religious service is usually conducted in the native language of the worshippers (in the United States, for example, English is used frequently in the service).

Conservative Judaism also started in the nineteenth century. Followers agree with the practices of Reform Judaism, but are strict on certain religious issues. They retain many Jewish traditions while recognizing the need for changes and adaptation to modern life. For example, although head coverings are required in the synagogue, men and women worship together and services are conducted both in Hebrew and the native language of the worshippers.

Reconstructionists see Judaism as a civilization, with the synagogue functioning as the center for all aspects of Jewish community life. The Reconstructionist service is similar to that of Conservative Judaism: men and women worship together. Women may also become rabbis. Reconstructionism is not widely practiced in Israel.

Modern synagogues have an auditorium where worshippers gather; a pulpit, or *bimah* (BEE-mah), above which hangs an electric light that is never switched off to symbolize the eternal light of the Torah; and a Holy Ark, where the scrolls of the Torah, the holiest scriptures, are kept.

THE TORAH AND THE TALMUD

The word Torah *means "to teach" in Hebrew. The Torah consists of the first five books of the Hebrew Bible. Also known as the Pentateuch, the Torah is made up of the books of Genesis, Exodus, Leviticus, Numbers, and Deuteronomy, and contains the entire body of traditional Jewish religious teaching and study. Moses is credited with writing the Torah, having received inspiration from God at Mount Sinai.*

In the synagogue, the Torah is in the form of a parchment scroll and is considered sacred. It is covered by specially decorated rich fabric.

The Talmud is a collection of sixty-three books of writings by ancient rabbis and discussions of the classification of religious and civil law by generations of scholars. It is also concerned with every aspect of Jewish life because Jewish religion and community are so closely related. There are two versions of the Talmud: the Palestinian Talmud and the Babylonian Talmud.

Synagogues must have windows, for they are considered retreats for life rather than retreats from life. Many temples have a washbasin and pitcher in the lobby, so that worshipers can pour water over their hands as an act of cleansing. All synagogues face toward Jerusalem.

CHRISTIANITY

The Christians of Israel represent several branches of Christendom and live mainly in the towns of Jerusalem, Bethlehem, Nazareth, Haifa, and Yafo. Among the most common Christian communities in Israel are the Eastern Orthodox, Roman Catholic, Armenian, Eastern Catholic, Syrian Orthodox, and Evangelical.

As a rule, each community is headed by a patriarch or archbishop who is assisted by an advisory council. Israel's Christian communities have their headquarters in Jerusalem, where the revered Church of the Holy Sepulcher is located. This house of worship is equally sacred to all Christian denominations, but it is mainly controlled by the Armenian, Greek Orthodox, and Roman Catholic churches.

The most ancient of these church groups in the Holy Land is the Greek Orthodox, which emerged before the middle of the second century. It gained importance during the reign of Emperor Constantine from 324 to 337 CE.

ISLAM

Islam is the religion of Muslims, who make up the second largest religious group in Israel. According to Islamic belief, the angel Gabriel appeared to the Prophet Muhammad and told him to teach God's words to the world. Muhammad preached in the seventh century that there is only one God, named Allah, and that he, Muhammad, was the final messenger of God. His companions memorized and recorded his revelations. These eventually became the holy writings of the Qur'an.

Muslims believe that there is one God, and that Muhammad is his prophet, and that there will be a judgment day. Muslims pray five times a day, facing the holy city of Mecca in Saudi Arabia. Prayer time is announced by a crier, or *muezzin* (moo-EH-zin), from a *minaret*, or tower in the mosque. The head of the mosque is an *imam* (i-MAHM), who leads people in prayer.

The mosque is the most important building for Muslims. The word mosque comes from the Arabic word *masjid* (MAHS-jid), or "place of prostration to God." Within the mosque, there is a *mihrab* (MIH-rahb), or prayer niche that points toward Mecca, a pulpit for the preacher, and a reading stand on which the Qur'an is placed. Most mosques have a minaret, a courtyard for washing before prayer, and a *madrasah* (MAH-drah-sah), or religious school.

Drinking liquor, gambling, and eating pork are forbidden in Islam. During the holy month of Ramadan, adult Muslims must go without eating or drinking from sunrise to sunset. A pilgrimage to Mecca is required at least once in a person's lifetime. Charity is also a requirement; Muslims must give a certain percentage of their wealth or income to the needy.

JUDAISM, CHRISTIANITY, AND ISLAM

The major religions of Israel all grew from the same source, the events described in the Hebrew Bible. There is no one Bible; there are various versions depending on the religion and denomination, but they all share some of the same content. The writings were composed mainly in Hebrew by various men, and were compiled and edited over the course of 1000 years.

These writings detail the history of the Israelites and their relationship with God. Their story begins with Abraham; therefore Judaism, Christianity, and Islam are called the Abrahamic religions. Today about 54 percent of the world's people belong to one of the Abrahamic religions. All three are monotheistic, meaning their belief is in one God.

 Judaism: *There are about 14 million Jews in the world. Jews refer to the Supreme Being by several names in Hebrew, primarily* Adonai, *(AD-un-eye). In English, the word is usually God or Lord. Jews believe in the coming of a Messiah, but mainly focus on the purpose of Earthly life and one's duties to God and fellow human beings. The Jewish Sabbath is Saturday, beginning at sundown on Friday and ending at sundown on Saturday.*

Christianity: *There are about 2 billion Christians in the world. Christians call the Hebrew Bible the Old Testament, and add to it a second section of writings called the New Testament, which detail the life and teachings of Jesus Christ. Christians believe that Jesus of Nazareth, a Jew, was the promised Messiah, the Son of God made flesh. They believe God is expressed in three manifestations: God the Father; God the Son, which is Jesus Christ; and God the Holy Spirit. This is called the Trinity. Christians also believe in an afterlife. The soul either unites with God (heaven) or not (hell) as a result of the person's actions during his or her life. The Christian Sabbath is Sunday.*

Islam: *There are about 1.3 billion Muslims in the world. Their holy book, the Qur'an, relates many stories that are similar to those in the Old Testament, particularly in regard to Abraham. Muslims believe God, or Allah, spoke to Muhammad, whom they regard as the final prophet. Muhammad lived in the seventh century* CE, *in what is today Saudi Arabia. He recorded Allah's revelations, and they became the Qur'an. Muslims believe Jesus was a prophet, but not the Messiah. The Muslim Sabbath is Friday.*

Like all religions, Islam has sects. Most Israeli Muslims belong to the Sunni sect. They believe that after Muhammad's death, leadership passed to the successors of Muhammad's clan. Shia Muslims, the second-largest sect, believe that leadership passed on to the descendants of Muhammad's son-in-law.

DRUZE

Druze is an offshoot of Islam. The Druze derive their name from Muhammad al-Darazi, a founder of the sect. While this community speaks Arabic and their outward social patterns are not too different from those of other people in the area, they are distinguished by a strong sense of cultural loyalty and unity. There is an effective ban on intermarriage and conversion of non-Druze to the sect that further separates this community from other Arabs. The Druze faction originated around 1000 BCE but only gained official recognition in Israel in 1957.

A long colonnade leads to a Baha'i temple in Haifa.

Druze beliefs and rituals remain largely secret. It is known, however, that the people believe in a god that operates through a system of five cosmic principles and that there are periodic human appearances of the deity. The Druze divide members of their faith into two groups: those who know the beliefs completely and those who do not. The first group consists of fewer than 10 percent of the total Druze population.

BAHA'I

The Baha'i faith was established in the mid-1800s in what is now Iraq. The efforts of Mirza Ali Muhammad, a nineteenth-century Persian mystic, are the inspiration behind this religion.

THE DEAD SEA SCROLLS

In 1947, a young Bedouin shepherd who was exploring a cave made one of the greatest archaeological finds in history. In this cave in the cliffs overlooking the Dead Sea, he found a set of parchment and papyrus scrolls containing religious writings that had been preserved in earthenware jars for nearly 2,000 years.

The recovered documents, now known as the Dead Sea Scrolls, were written by the ancient Hebrews who lived on what is now the site of Qumran. Thought to be members of the Essene sect, this devoutly religious group hid its sacred writings in the cave in anticipation of war with the Romans around 66 CE. The Essene community was destroyed, but its writings remained, safely hidden through the ages.

After the initial discovery, archaeological digs unearthed additional scrolls and fragments in eleven other caves. Years of study and careful reconstruction revealed the history of a community that removed itself from typical Jewish life, following a "teacher of righteousness" into the wilderness.

The scrolls tell much about the history of Jews, early Christianity, and the Bible. Some were written in Hebrew, while others were written in Aramaic, the language spoken in that region at the time. Approximately one-fourth of the scrolls are biblical writings; each book of the Old Testament, except the book of Esther, is represented. A complete copy of the book of Isaiah was found, and it is believed to be the oldest copy.

The Dead Sea Scrolls are currently housed at the Shrine of the Book in Jerusalem, a museum devoted to these manuscripts.

According to the Baha'i, a series of prophets were sent to teach moral truths and social principles. The last of these prophets was Baha'u'llah. Baha'u'llah proclaimed the importance of all religions worshipping one God, and that service to other human beings is the most significant act. He also said that God wants a united society based on mutual love and acceptance, and stressed moral and social improvement.

The international governing body of the faith, the Universal House of Justice, meets in Haifa.

INTERNET LINKS

www.jewfaq.org/index.shtml
Judaism 101
Answers to questions about Judaism.

www.smithsonianmag.com/history/who-wrote-the-dead-sea-scrolls-11781900/?no-ist
Smithsonian Magazine: "Who Wrote the Dead Sea Scrolls?"
A fascinating article about the scholarly debate over the authorship of the Dead Sea Scrolls.

www.aish.com/jw/s/48892792.html
Aish.com: "Why Jews Don't Believe In Jesus"
This article answers a question that can help Christians understand the Jewish position.

www.religionfacts.com/islam/comparison_charts/islam_judaism_christianity.htm
Religion Facts: Comparison of Islam, Judaism, and Christianity
This excellent site offers at-a-glance charts comparing the basic facts, origins, and beliefs of the three religions.

LANGUAGE

An orthodox Jewish man prays at the Western Wall using a scroll of Hebrew writing.

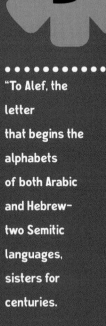

9

HEBREW IS THE ONLY LANGUAGE IN history to have been brought back from the dead and used as a national language. A dead language is one that is no longer spoken in everyday use, though it may still exist in old texts and liturgical ceremonies. Latin is one such language. Hebrew had not been spoken as a native tongue by anyone for centuries. Today it is the native tongue of millions of people.

Israel has two official languages: Hebrew and Arabic. Hebrew is the mother tongue of approximately 60 percent of the population. Arabic is spoken by Arabs and many older Jews from Arab countries. Yiddish is spoken mostly by older Ashkenazim and Ultra-Orthodox Jews.

Arabic is taught in Israel's Arab schools and used in legal affairs and in the legislature. French is also taught in most schools. English is a *lingua franca* in Israel, which means that it is used as a common or commercial language among people who do not speak the same language. In fact, money, postage stamps, and road signs are printed in English as well as in Hebrew and Arabic, and English is a compulsory subject in schools. Very few Israelis speak only one language.

HEBREW

Hebrew is one of the world's oldest extant languages. For more than 2,000 years Hebrew has been the religious language of Jews and, at

"To Alef, the letter that begins the alphabets of both Arabic and Hebrew— two Semitic languages, sisters for centuries.

May we find the language that takes us to the only home there is— one another's hearts."
—Ibtisam Barakat, from *Tasting the Sky: A Palestinian Childhood*, 2007

THE HEBREW ALPHABET

The Hebrew alphabet consists of twenty-two letters, Alef *through* Tav. *Five of these have a different form when they appear at the end of a word. It is quite different from the English alphabet, for it has no capital letters or vowels.*

In the eighth century, a system was developed for indicating vowels through the use of dots and dashes. These signs, called diacritics, are found in all printed editions of the Hebrew Bible.

Only when a word is part of a sentence can the reader know the intended meaning. Hebrew, like most Semitic languages, is read from right to left.

times, their spoken language. There are two main branches of Hebrew: Ashkenasic from Central Europe; and Sephardic from the Mediterranean region. The difference between the two is in the pronunciation of certain letters. Sephardic Hebrew is used in Israel.

Like any language, Hebrew has undergone changes throughout its history, but unlike most, there were not many changes until the modern period. The main reason for this is that Hebrew was not spoken, except in prayer, from the time the Jews were driven from Israel in the second century until the beginning of the twentieth century.

Although the spoken language has changed by acquiring the thousands of words needed to become functional in the modern world, the written language has remained quite unchanged. In fact, today's Israeli high-school student can easily read and understand the original text of the Bible. The revival of Hebrew after 1,800 years of inactivity was due largely to the enormous work of Eliezer Ben-Yehuda, who moved to Israel in 1881.

Ben-Yehuda was responsible for the relentless task of creating modern words from ancient Hebrew roots. But without the cooperation of the Jews of Palestine, who eventually began to speak the language, Hebrew would have remained only a scriptural language.

Cooperation was slow in coming, however. At first, Orthodox rabbis denounced the attempt as dishonoring the scriptures, and Zionist leader Theodor Herzl felt that speaking the language was not practical. Because language is closely tied to a culture's identity, the Jews of the world who were returning to their homeland finally accepted that Hebrew would be a unifying force. What made the acceptance of Hebrew successful was that Ben-Yehuda adapted the ancient written language for modern use. This allowed the millions of present and future immigrants to master the language easily and quickly.

Ben-Yehuda published a Hebrew newspaper and a sixteen-volume standard dictionary. In addition, he gathered a group of scholars to form a council, known today as the Hebrew Language Academy, or *Vaad Ha-Lashon*, to develop modern words. The academy continues to search the Bible and ancient Hebrew texts for words they can adapt to modern meanings. For example, for the word *babysitter*, they combined the words *young child* and *guard*.

When Ben-Yehuda started speaking Hebrew just over 100 years ago, it had a limited vocabulary. Today, Hebrew consists of more than 100,000 words, largely because of the tireless efforts of the Vaad Ha-Lashon. Words borrowed from other languages have also greatly contributed to the Hebrew lexicon.

ARABIC

Arabic is the mother tongue of about 300 million Middle Eastern people, spoken in a broad belt from the Arabian Peninsula all the way to the Atlantic Ocean. It is the language of Islam and the Qur'an and, in 1974, was named the sixth official language of the United Nations.

Hebrew and Arabic are languages in the Semitic language family. They have similar alphabet systems and word and sentence structural styles.

Spoken Arabic varies across countries and may be mutually unintelligible from one country or region to another. However, classical Arabic (the

language of the Qur'an) has remained essentially unchanged since the seventh century and provides a common platform for Arabic-speaking people of different countries to communicate.

The alphabet consists of twenty-eight letters, which are basically consonants. Vowel signs, as in Hebrew, are indicated by marks above and below the letters. Typical of Semitic languages, Arabic is read from right to left.

YIDDISH

Yiddish, spoken by many older Ashkenazim Israelis until about sixty years ago, was the language of the Jews of Eastern and Central Europe. It is a German dialect that is written in Hebrew characters. Vowels, however, are written in Yiddish.

This language arose around the ninth century as Jews adapted German to their needs, adding Hebrew words that were a part of their religious life. As Jews migrated eastward, Yiddish picked up Slavic influences. The language greatly reflects its culture: there are few terms descriptive of nature, which Eastern European Jews had little contact with, and it is loaded with descriptive terms of character and about relations between people. Yiddish continues to be spoken by ultra-Orthodox Jews in Israel as they feel it is wrong to use Hebrew as an everyday language.

ISRAELI NAMES

A clear indication of how Hebrew has come to represent the Zionist spirit is evident in Israeli names. So eager were many Jews to become a part of their homeland that they took new Hebrew last names. Those who were able to translate their names into Hebrew did so.

People named Schneider (German for "tailor") became *Hayati*, Weiss (German for "white") was changed to *Livni* for instance and so on. Others chose last names representing their favorite regions, such as *Galili* (Galilee), *Negbi* (Negev), or *Yerushalmi* (Jerusalem).

Many newcomers selected surnames symbolic of their self-image or after their parents or children. *Avigad* is a common Israeli last name that simply means "father of Gad." Eliezer Ben-Yehuda was Eliezer Perelman before emigrating to Palestine. There, he preferred to be known as "son of Judea." *Ami*, *Avi*, *Bat*, or *Ben* at the beginning of last names mean "mother of," "father of," "daughter of," and "son of" respectively.

Others who took Hebrew surnames included prime ministers such as David Ben-Gurion (who was previously David Green) and Golda Meir (Goldie Meyerson). Ben-Gurion felt so strongly about this that he made changing of names to Hebrew a requirement for public servants and government officials.

Biblical first names such as Benjamin, Naomi, Esther, David, and Ezra remain popular. However, many people are naming their children after beautiful Hebrew words. Names such as *Ayala* (deer), *Dafna* (laurel), *Orli* (my light), *Ari* (lion), *Eitan* (strong, firm), and *Gad* (fortune) are some of the names becoming more common.

INTERNET LINKS

www.omniglot.com/writing/hebrew.htm
Omniglot is an online encyclopedia of writing systems and languages.

www.zigzagworld.com/hebrewforme
ZigZag World: Hebrew for Me
A site for learning the Hebrew language.

www.al-bab.com/arab/language/lang.htm
Al Bab
Information about the Arabic language.

www.jewfaq.org/yiddish.htm
Judaism 101: Yiddish Language and Culture
An amusing and interesting in-depth overview of Yiddish.

ARTS

This aerial view shows the stunning architecture of the wedge-shaped Yad Vashem, the Holocaust Museum in Jerusalem.

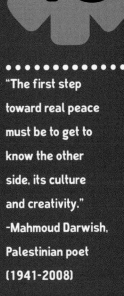

10

JEWISH ART AND ARCHITECTURE date back to ancient times. From the time Moses asked Bezalel to craft a gold menorah and an ark for the Ten Commandments, the Jewish people have made beautiful jewelry, pottery, and on a larger scale, temples and castles.

Today's artists, both Jewish and Arab, have much to inspire them. The span of old and new, the conflict of cultures, the political strife, and the personal life stories that haunt Israel's collective memory—all produce a deep, richly layered atmosphere that sparks creativity.

Israel has more museums per capita—meaning for the size of its population—than any other country. That is one indication of the importance of arts and culture to these people. Though many of the more than 200 museums are not dedicated to art, the majority of them are. The Israel Museum in Jerusalem is the largest; the Museum of Art, Ein Harod, Israel's first museum, was built on a kibbutz. There's the Museum for Islamic Art in Jerusalem for ancient Islamic works, and the new Umm el-Fahem Art Gallery that showcases the contemporary art of Arabs and Palestinians.

Some of the buildings housing these museums are works of art in themselves, such as the new wing of the Tel Aviv Museum of Art, the Design Museum Holon, and Yad Vashem, the Holocaust Museum in Jerusalem. The Yad Vashem isn't strictly an art museum, though it includes one, but the building itself is one of Israel's most compelling architectural masterpieces—a graceful concrete triangular form that penetrates a mountain from one side to the other.

In 1991, during the Gulf War, the Israel Philharmonic Orchestra played a concert wearing gas masks as scud missiles fired by Iraq fell on Tel Aviv.

THE PERFORMING ARTS

Music has contributed greatly to the cultural advancement and international reputation of Israel. The Israel Philharmonic Orchestra, founded in 1936, has had many famous musicians and conductors among its ranks. These include Isaac Stern and Itzak Perlman, two violinists who are known the world over for their musical talent. Israelis are tremendously devoted to the philharmonic orchestra. It is one of the most widely supported orchestras (per capita) in the world. It is even said that some residents of Tel Aviv read the obituaries in hopes of recognizing the name of someone they knew to be a ticket holder, which would provide an opportunity for a seat.

Israel's music in the early years of statehood was very much in the folk tradition, with a biblical focus. It has since shifted away from the religious and toward the political. Described as sad but optimistic, it touches on the things that are on the minds of the Israelis, such as peace and war.

The many cultural groups that have come together have blended to create

The Israel Philharmonic Orchestra, which predates the modern country, draws a large audience at a convention center in Jerusalem.

a musical form that is distinctly Israeli. One popular singer, Ofra Haza, even recorded a sixteenth-century Yemenite prayer, sung to rap music; it sold more than a million units worldwide.

Israelis also love the theater. There are five major acting companies in the country, and Israelis lead the world in per-capita theater attendance. Habima, the national theater company, has been producing plays since 1932. It performs three times daily, six days a week, to near-capacity crowds. Beersheba, Jerusalem, and Haifa have repertory acting companies, and community theaters flourish throughout the land, including on the kibbutz.

LITERATURE

There has been a continuous Hebrew literary tradition even though the language was not spoken except in religious services from the second century until the late nineteenth century.

Most literary works that emerged soon after Israel was created in 1948 were by writers who took part in the Palmach, an elite strike force set up in 1941. These writers wrote about war and heroism. Haim Gouri and Moshe Shamir are among the writers who belong to this generation.

Israeli literature addressed personal issues in the 1950s and 1960s, as writers such as Amos Oz, Aaron Applefeld, and A. B. Yehoshua reflected on the struggles of individuals and families in a young state, the Holocaust, and the gathering and absorbing of Jews of various ethnic groups in Israel. Perhaps the best-known writer of this group, S. Y. Agnon, won the 1966 Nobel Prize for Literature for his fictional works.

The 1980s saw a revolution in Israeli literature. A large number of young writers emerged with original works during this period, and there was a greater variety of books from different and new genres. Recent literary works have moved away from taking moral or ideological stands, and resemble the themes of Western writing.

As works by Israeli Arab writers are usually in Arabic, they have not joined the mainstream body of literature in Israel, most of which is in Hebrew. Their works have not gone uncredited, however. Emil Habibi is an Israeli Arab writer who won the Israel Prize, while Anton Shammas is an Israeli

Christian Arab recognized for his 1986 *Arabesques*, one of the first Israeli Arab literary works.

Over the past six decades, Israeli literature has evolved from focusing on ideological and Zionist issues to addressing personal experiences.

VISUAL ARTS

Israelis are fond of art. Original artwork can often be found in even the smallest apartment. There are countless art galleries in the cities—especially Tel Aviv—and for a country of its size, Israel has many museums. These museums are found in cities and even on the kibbutz, housing treasures of archaeology and local history, ancient and modern works, and primitive and sophisticated craftworks.

An attempt at creating an Israeli style in painting was started by the Bezalel School of Arts and Crafts, which was founded in Jerusalem in 1906. The style combined traditional Jewish themes and images with modern Western concepts, but over the years, newness and originality have been the major element in Israeli art.

Ballet students dance in a performance in Netania.

DANCE

Dance has always been an integral part of Jewish life. There are many biblical references to it as an expression of joy and religious excitement, and there are various traditional Jewish dances incorporated into many types of ceremonies.

The various ethnic groups that have emigrated to the Holy Land brought many dance forms, among them the *debka* (DAB-kah), which is an Arabic

THE INBAL DANCE THEATER

The Inbal Dance Theater celebrates traditions of the Yemenite Jews, who were isolated from mainstream Judaism for 2,000 years. The music and dance forms that the Yemenite Jews brought to their new home are reminders of ancient religious rituals and ceremonies. Yemenite music and storytelling accompany the traditional dance movements, which include rhythmic walking, exciting head and body movements, and captivating hand gestures. The group also incorporated Jewish folkloric materials from a range of Israel's subcultures, including the Yemenite, Moroccan, Kurdish, Persian, Hasidic, and Arab. Based in Tel Aviv, the Inbal Dance Theater is regarded as a national cultural treasure and receives international acclaim.

line dance performed by men, and the *hora* (HORE-uh), an Eastern European circle dance. In many traditional dances, there is strict separation of the sexes in dance, so participants hold the ends of a handkerchief to prevent physical contact.

Community folk dancing is a part of modern Israeli culture. After the sabbath on Saturday evenings, many Israelis join in folk dancing in local parks and on the kibbutzim.

The Industrial Engineering and Management building at the Technion in Haifa is an example of new Israeli architecture.

Professional dance groups are heavily supported in Israel. There are three major modern dance institutions, professional folk-dance groups, and even a hearing-impaired dancers' troupe.

ARCHITECTURE

In Israel, all styles of architecture combine. From the traditional Arab-style villas that blend into the surrounding landscape, and the simple tile-roofed houses of the first settlers, to the modern European forms of seaside cottages.

Following the post-World War I and post-World War II mass immigrations, the *shikkun* (shi-KOON), or housing project, became necessary to accommodate the increase in population, with an emphasis on usefulness rather than beauty. Nonetheless, since statehood, Israeli architects have attempted to introduce style and grace into new institutions. Higher education campuses led the way in the creation of structures with a style that could be characterized as Israel. The Hebrew University Givat Ram campus in Jerusalem, the Technion in Haifa, and the Weizmann Institute in Rehovot are all examples of beautifully designed, highly functional buildings.

Other public buildings with notable architecture are the Israel Museum Complex in Jerusalem, the Knesset, various concert halls, and the Jerusalem and Haifa theaters.

INTERNET LINKS

ww.goisrael.com
The Israel Ministry of Tourism site has information on music, visual arts, dance, museums, and more. Click on Art & Culture.

www.myjewishlearning.com/culture/2/Music/Israeli_Music/History. shtml
My Jewish Learning: Israeli Music History
An overview of the rich musical traditions in Israel.

www.english.imjnet.org.il
The Israel Museum, Jerusalem
This art and archaeology museum is the largest cultural institution in Israel.

www.tamuseum.org.il/collection-category/israeli-art
Tel Aviv Museum of Art
Modern and contemporary art of Israel.

www.redseajazzeilat.com/en
Red Sea Jazz Festival

www.ipo.co.il/eng/HomePage/.aspx
Israel Philharmonic Orchestra

LEISURE

People enjoy water sports in the Gulf of Aqaba in the Red Sea, off the coast of Eilat, Israel

11

F ROM HANGING OUT WITH FRIENDS, grabbing some fast food, catching a movie, or shopping at the mall, to cheering on a favorite team, leisure time in Israel is much the same as in the United States. One difference is that pretty much everything, including public transportation, shuts down on Friday evenings and Saturday, the Jewish sabbath. Another difference is that Israelis work and go to school six days a week. Their one day off is the sabbath, so time for fun is limited.

The most popular leisure activity in Israel is visiting. On weekday evenings, people visit friends and family. Adults get together quite often for coffee and cake. On Friday evenings, even the least religious of Jewish families have their version of the traditional sabbath dinner.

IN PURSUIT OF LEISURE

There is a strong emphasis on physical fitness in Israel, as most Jewish citizens serve in the military for a few years and remain on call for reservist training for some time after. So traditional sports, as well as outdoor or nature activities such as hiking, are popular leisure pursuits.

Many people say Tel Aviv is Israel's most fun city, with exciting night life, gorgeous beaches, fancy restaurants, and great shopping. One of the city's top attractions is the acclaimed new Nalaga'at Center, featuring a theater company of blind/deaf actors and the Blackout Restaurant where everyone dines in pitch darkness, served by blind waiters.

Much of the Israelis' free time is spent outdoors. People love to go out to eat. Food vendors are everywhere, offering a variety of international fast foods from the Middle Eastern *falafel* (fuh-LAH-fehl), or spicy ground chickpea balls, to New York-style hot dogs. Outdoor cafés are very popular. While enjoying cups of iced coffee, many people get together to play chess and backgammon or argue about politics and world affairs.

As in any country, some of the types of leisure activities that the inhabitants enjoy are determined by locality. Some interests that are shared by all Israelis are reading, going to the movies, watching television, listening to the radio, and attending concerts and the ballet.

SPORTS

Sports have become increasingly important in Israel in recent years. There are many sports clubs as well as facilities and equipment provided for the population by both the government and private organizations.

Soccer is by far Israel's favorite sport; all activity seems to stop on the

Young men play soccer, or football, on a beach in Ashdod.

THE MACCABIAH GAMES

Every four years, Israel hosts the Maccabiah Games, an Olympics-style sporting event for Jewish athletes from around the world. The goal of the games is to bring Jews together in the Holy Land and to promote physical excellence and well-being. In 2013 Israel hosted the Nineteenth Maccabiah Games. Team USA sent a delegation of 1,100 athletes to the games, and there were athletes from seventy-six countries in all. The games are open to all Jews as well as all Israelis, regardless of religion.

Joseph Yekutieli founded the Maccabiah Games in 1932. In the first games, approximately 500 athletes from twenty-three countries participated, and many later remained in Palestine to become citizens. For the second Maccabiah Games in 1935, nearly 2,000 athletes came. However, the third games did not take place until 1950, first postponed because of World War II, and later due to the establishment of the state of Israel.

Today, events include table tennis, basketball, volleyball, track and field, tennis, boxing, soccer, swimming, water polo, gymnastics, fencing, and wrestling—all of the Olympic events, plus even more. Like the Olympics, the Maccabiah Games have dramatic and moving opening and closing ceremonies, which are attended by top Israeli officials.

afternoon of an important soccer match. Spectators tend to become quite involved in the game, especially if they do not agree with an important decision by the referee. Israel has a soccer team that competes internationally and a national league, in which teams compete against one another on a regular basis.

Basketball is growing in popularity. One Israeli team, Maccabi Tel Aviv, has twice captured the European Cup championship. It has also crossed the Atlantic to play exhibition games against the American NBA teams. In Israel there is also a twelve-team professional league with many U.S.-born players.

Interest in tennis is growing by leaps and bounds. The country's climate is perfect for outdoor activity throughout the year, and there are tennis courts and stadiums in most cities and towns. Two Israeli professional tennis players, Shlomo Glickstein and Amos Mansdorf, have been ranked among the top competitors in the world. Among the country's top players, Shahar Pe'er has led the pack in recent years among both male and female competitors.

Hiking is a great national passion. On Saturday afternoons, countless families pack into their cars and set out for national parks for a picnic and to explore the country on foot. An organized annual springtime hiking event that is a three-day march through the hills of Judea and Samaria has attracted participants ranging from teenagers to people in their seventies. Those who finish the march parade victoriously through Jerusalem.

TELEVISION

Israelis love to watch television not just for entertainment but for newscasts, which provide important information for a country where dramatic events occur often. The length of the newscast depends on the amount of news, but on an average day, it runs for thirty minutes. Apart from the news, Israelis enjoy the same type of television entertainment as do North Americans. In fact, much of Israeli television fare is imported from the United States.

Israeli television is mainly broadcast on one channel. Educational programs, such as the Hebrew version of Sesame Street and cartoons are aired from morning until about 5 p.m. Arabic television follows the educational broadcasts. For three hours, the Israeli Arab minority, residents of the occupied territories, and any Arab in the neighboring countries who is interested, tune in to the Arabic news and other Arabic programs. Israelis can also watch Jordanian and Syrian television because the Middle Eastern electronic media have no national boundaries.

American programs are very popular and are aired after the Arabic programs. Israeli TV also imports programs from Europe, Canada, and Australia. Israel also produces plenty of its own shows, from sitcoms to dramas to *Rising Star*, an *American Idol*-style singing competition. There are no commercials on Israeli TV.

RADIO

Radio is also an Israeli passion. Bus drivers turn up the volume of the hourly newscasts so that passengers can hear all the latest news; and during times of great crisis, Israelis are never without radios by their side.

Israel has a major news station that employs the finest journalists, who are constantly interviewing top Israeli officials such as the prime minister and giving reports and commentaries on economic and international news. There is also a military radio station that not only presents four newscasts daily, but also plays jazz and rock music.

The Israeli Broadcasting Authority broadcasts programs for local and overseas listeners in sixteen languages, including Hebrew, Arabic, English, French, Russian, and Spanish. It gears its programming to the needs of Israel's immigrants. The musical tastes of the young and old are also satisfied. One station beats out rock tunes all day long and into the night, while another may be dedicated to classical music that soothes thousands with its eighteen hours of broadcasting each day.

INTERNET LINKS

www.haaretz.com
Israel news covers a wide range of topics, plus opinion, lifestyle, and even archaeology news.

www.maccabiah.com
The home page of the Maccabiah Games.

eng.football.org.il/Pages/default.aspx
The Israel Football Association
Home page of the men's and women's national soccer teams.

www.nalagaat.org.il/home.php
The Nalaga'at Center home page provides an overview of this unique arts foundation.

FESTIVALS

An ultra-Orthodox man plays the violin during a Purim celebration in Jerusalem.

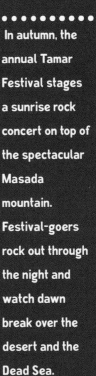

12

ISRAEL IS A LIVELY PLACE, ESPECIALLY in the summer time. In the big cities and small towns, festivals bring people outside to enjoy the arts, culture, and just about anything imaginable. There's the amazing Jerusalem Festival, a celebration of all things Jerusalem—arts, music, theater, food, dance, parties, ideas, history, films, parks, private homes, holy sites, and more. There's the Jacob's Ladder Music Festival on the shores of the Sea of Galilee, the Guitar Festival of the Desert in the Negev, and the Red Sea Jazz Festival in Eilat, to name a few.

The word *festival* brings to mind a joyous celebration, and the music and arts festivals are joyous indeed. Many major Jewish holidays, however, have a more somber and reflective tone as people commemorate major historical events. In Israel, holy land to three of the world's great religions, people celebrate festivals that range from religious to secular and from solemn to exuberant.

In autumn, the annual Tamar Festival stages a sunrise rock concert on top of the spectacular Masada mountain. Festival-goers rock out through the night and watch dawn break over the desert and the Dead Sea.

JEWISH HOLIDAYS

Since ancient times, Jewish people have cherished and observed their holy days. The rituals were a uniting force for the Jews of the Diaspora, and the holidays themselves served as reminders of their strong leadership and exceptional circumstances. Some of the holidays celebrated in Israel originated more than 3,000 years ago. Over the years, as they met great challenges, they added more memorable days to their festivals calendar.

THE HIGH HOLY DAYS

Rosh Hashanah and Yom Kippur mark the beginning of the Jewish year. According to tradition, God opens three books on Rosh Hashanah—one for the wicked, one for the righteous, and one for all others. The names of the righteous are written in the Book of Life; the wicked are designated for death in the coming year; and judgment on the rest is suspended for a ten-day period of personal accounting and atonement that occurs between Rosh

Israeli soldiers bless a plate of apple and honey to welcome Rosh Hashanah, the Jewish New Year. The custom symbolizes the prayer for a sweet year ahead.

Israelis live their daily lives by a solar calendar, which starts with the month of January and ends with December. This is known as the Gregorian calendar. However, Israelis mark the dates of their national and religious holidays on a lunar calendar that starts with the month of Tishri *and ends with* Elul. *This is known as the Hebrew calendar. If the date is April 12, 2014 on the Gregorian calendar, it is* Nisan 12, 5774, *on the Hebrew calendar. The* Jerusalem Post *prints both the Gregorian and the Hebrew dates every day.*

The twelve Hebrew months begin with the appearance of the new moon, and each month has twenty-nine or thirty days. To prevent the lunar year from slipping too far behind the solar year, every few years an extra month, called Adar Bet *or* Adar II, *is added.*

The Islamic calendar also has twelve months that begin with the new moon. However, it does not make an attempt to relate the lengths of the solar and lunar years, and a holiday that occurs in summer one year can fall in winter years later. If a Gregorian date, for example April 12, falls in the Islamic month of Jumaada al-Thaany *in the year 2014, (or 1435 on the Islamic calendar), the same date would have fallen in a different Islamic month,* Safar, *a decade earlier in 2004 (1425 on the Islamic calendar).*

Following a lunar year schedule can have some very interesting results. For example, when Israel celebrated its independence on May 14 in 1948, it was the fifth day of the Hebrew month of Iyar, which did not coincide with May 14 again until the year 2005. The next time that will happen will be in 2024.

Hashanah and Yom Kippur. A typical greeting among Jews during this holiday season is, "May you be inscribed in the Book of Life."

ROSH HASHANAH falls in September or October. While the holiday has a serious overtone, the new year is welcomed with a sense of joy. After attending services at the synagogue, Jewish families gather for a festive meal. Jewish delicacies are prepared as symbols of good luck. The following night, fruits of the season are eaten for the first time in the new year. This holiday is extremely popular because it is the only one in the entire year that is observed for two consecutive days. Apart from worshiping, Israelis take advantage of the break by making trips to the beach, organizing picnics and barbecues, or hiking in the country's national parks.

YOM KIPPUR On Yom Kippur, Jews make their peace with God and their conscience. It is said that one's fate is written on Rosh Hashanah and sealed on Yom Kippur by God. Judgment is made after an appropriate period of soul-searching and asking for forgiveness from God.

Yom Kippur has been observed since the days of Moses. On this solemn day, Jews refrain from eating and drinking to atone for the sins of the past year. Their fast begins at sundown on the eve of Yom Kippur and ends at sundown on Yom Kippur with a large meal shared by the whole family.

Sukkot are built on the balconies of homes in the Old City of Jerusalem.

SUKKOT

Shortly after the High Holy Days, traditional Jews celebrate *Sukkot*, the Harvest Festival, over a period of eight days. Families build a *sukkah* (SOO-kah), or hut, next to their homes, representing the dwelling of the ancient Jews who wandered the desert after their escape from Egypt.

Sukkot is the most visible festival in Israel. Even secular Jews build the sukkah. In their case, however, the sukkah symbolizes the Diaspora. Israelis who celebrate the religious aspect of Sukkot eat their meals in the sukkah in thanksgiving at the close of the harvest season.

Simchat Torah ("Rejoicing of the Torah") falls on the last day of Sukkot and is celebrated with dancing, singing, and worship. It coincides with the completion of the reading of the Torah for the year. In the synagogue, a

Name of festival	Month it usually falls in Gregorian calendar
Tu B'Shvat (New Year for Trees)	January or February
Purim (Feast of Lots)	February or March
Pesach (Passover)	March or April
Yom Ha'Shoah (Holocaust Memorial Day)	April or May
Yom Ha'Zikaron (Israel Memorial Day)	April or May
Yom Ha'atzmaut (Israel Independence Day)	April or May
Yom Yerushalayim (Jerusalem Day)	
Shavuot	May or June
Rosh Hashanah (New Year)	September or October
Yom Kippur (Day of Atonement)	September or October
Sukkot (Festival of Tabernacles) (Harvest Festival)	September or October
Simchat Torah (Rejoicing of the Torah)	September or October
Hanukkah (Festival of Lights)	November or December

parade precedes a ceremonial unrolling of a Torah scroll to the first chapter, and the reading of the first five books of the Bible begins anew.

HANUKKAH

Hanukkah is an eight-day festival that celebrates the victory of Judah Maccabee's warriors over the Syrians, who tried to convert their religion in the second century BCE. Upon victory, the Jews set out to rededicate the temple in Jerusalem, only to find that there was just enough oil to burn for one day. However, the oil miraculously burned for eight days.

To celebrate this miracle, Jews burn candles on the *hanukkiah*, a special menorah with nine candle holders used in Hanukkah celebrations. One

A family lights all of the special candles on the final night of Hanukkah.

candle is lit on each of the festival's eight nights. The ninth candle, called *shamash*, or servant candle, is the first to be lit and used for lighting all the other candles.

Hanukkah is enjoyed widely in Israel; families gather to party and eat traditional Hanukkah foods, and children receive gifts from their parents on each of the eight nights. In the village of Modin, where the Maccabees came from, a special relay race commemorates the holiday. The first runner lights the torch of freedom and independence and carries it to the next runner. The passing of the torch goes on until the last runner reaches Jerusalem and hands the torch to the president of Israel.

PESACH

Pesach, or Passover, a springtime holiday, is a memorial of the Israelites' escape from hundreds of years of slavery in Egypt.

The word *passover* comes from the time when God sent an angel to slay the firstborn son of every Egyptian home, but passed over Jewish homes that were marked with blood from sacrificial lambs. The Egyptians were so overcome by the tragedy that the Jews were able to escape. The fleeing Jews had no time to wait for the bread they were baking to rise. Thus even today Jews observe a restriction against foods that rise (particularly, unleavened breads) and certain grains throughout Passover.

An important night during Pesach is the evening of the Seder, which is a ceremonial dinner on the first night of this seven-day festival. The Seder recreates the events of the escape, or exodus, from Egypt. A special storyline of the exodus called the *Hagadda* (HOG-ah-dah) is read aloud. Celebrants (especially children) participate by answering questions from the Hagadda and eating the symbolic foods for the ceremony.

This holiday is also celebrated by all Jews, as it is a festival of freedom. Yom Ha'Shoah, the Holocaust Memorial, is celebrated after Passover. Shavuot, the day God gave the Ten Commandments to the Israelites, is celebrated after Israel's Memorial Day and Independence Day.

A man places a poppy on the name of his relative at a memorial ceremony for fallen paratroopers.

MEMORIAL AND INDEPENDENCE

Independence Day celebrations are preceded by Memorial Day, when Israelis remember those who gave their lives for the state.

During Memorial Day, television and radio stations broadcast documentaries on Israeli battles and their heroes. During a two-minute silence, work stops while cars and buses wait at the side of the road. At sundown, sirens scream across the country and the Independence Day celebrations begin. Families build bonfires on the hillsides and people sit around the fires to sing and tell stories.

Christians follow the Via Dolorosa in Jerusalem on Good Friday. It is the route on which Jesus carried the cross on the day of his crucifixion.

CHRISTIAN HOLIDAYS

Like Christians everywhere, Israeli Christians celebrate Christmas, Good Friday, and Easter. During these holidays, church bells in the old section of Jerusalem ring, summoning Christians to walk where Jesus walked.

At Christmas, pilgrims gather around Manger Square in Bethlehem, while beautiful music pours out of the Church of the Nativity. Christians also look out for Baba Noel, as Santa Claus is known in Israel, and decorate their houses with Christmas trees.

Easter offers the most dramatic sight in Jerusalem, where hundreds of pilgrims make their way down Via Dolorosa during Holy Week. This is the route Jesus took to Calvary, where he was crucified.

ISLAMIC HOLIDAYS

The most joyous of Muslim holidays occurs at the end of the fasting month of Ramadan, when there is a three-day feast called Eid-al-Fitr. It is also a time for family visits. Sweet pastries are served and children receive gifts such as clothing. People also dye their hands with a natural orange-red dye called henna as a symbol of good luck.

Eid-al-Adha, the Feast of the Sacrifice, is also referred to as the "big holiday." It honors Ibrahim (Abraham) and his son Ismail. According to the Qur'an, God wanted to test Ibrahim's loyalty by commanding him to sacrifice his beloved son, Ismail. When Ibrahim relayed this command to Ismail, the latter encouraged his father to obey, out of their great love and faith in God. When the moment for Ismail's sacrifice came, however, God substituted a lamb in his place as a sign of his grace and power. Muslims sacrifice sheep, cows, or goats to remember this event. The meat is cooked in special festive dishes, with portions of it given to the poor. This holiday abounds with sweet pastries, henna, and gifts. Muslims who can afford it perform the pilgrimage to Mecca in Saudi Arabia during this period. This pilgrimage is one of the five pillars of Islam and should be performed at least once in a Muslim's lifetime according to the person's means.

INTERNET LINKS

www.chabad.org/holidays/default_cdo/jewish/holidays.htm
Jewish Holidays and Festivals
Links to full coverage of each of the Jewish holidays, including some lesser-known days.

www.timeanddate.com/holidays/israel
Time and Date lists holidays by country and by year.

www.touristisrael.com/events/festivals-in-israel
Tourist Israel offers a list of seasonal, cultural, and holiday festivals.

FOOD

Sufganiyot, or donuts filled with jam or chocolate, are a favorite Israeli treat.

• • • • • • • • • • • •
"The only thing
chicken about
Israel is their
soup."
-Bob Hope,
American
comedian
(1903-2003)

ISRAEL MAY BE A YOUNG NATION, BUT its cuisine has a long history. People from many parts of the world have settled in the country, bringing with them their favorite traditional recipes, which come from afar and are perhaps centuries old. Blending these varied culinary traditions, Israelis have developed a cuisine that they can now call their own.

It would not have been clear back in the 1940s whether an Israeli cuisine would emerge. With many more urgent matters to think about, cooking styles and methods did not seem all that important; food was an essential, something people needed in order to survive and get by. Today, however, many Israelis enjoy the art and experience of cooking with an ethnic flair.

ISRAELI FOODS

The foods eaten in Israel today are eclectic, coming from many cultures. Native Israeli cuisine might be described as similar to that of the Arab nations, but the Asian and European influences on the Israeli diet are unmistakable. Asian cuisine brings with it the flavor and aroma of distinctive spices and herbs, while European cuisine is relatively sweeter. Israeli cuisine combines the two with modern recipes.

The Israeli food tradition was formed according to the availability (or lack) of certain foods. For example, fruits and vegetables, which

Fragrant spices are on display at an open market.

are inexpensive and grown in large amounts, are included in virtually every meal. Dairy products, including different types of yogurt and soured milks and creams, are also a major part of the Israeli diet. Red meat is rarely eaten, partly because the lack of quality grazing land for livestock produces a lower grade of meat. Turkey and chicken are a major part of the Israeli diet.

The Jewish state's best contribution to world cuisine is undoubtedly the Israeli breakfast. This outstanding meal has its roots in the kibbutz. In the early morning hours, kibbutz farmers have a light snack consisting of tea with toast and jam so that they can get to the fields before the day gets hot. It is after putting in a few hours of hard work that they return for breakfast.

A typical Israeli breakfast, especially on the kibbutz, consists of vegetables such as tomatoes, onions, green peppers, and radishes; olives; eggs; carrot salad; a variety of dairy products, including buttermilk, yogurt, cottage cheese, and hard cheeses; breads; herring; hot cereals; and coffee or tea. It is served buffet-style and satisfies everyone's appetite.

For other meals, falafel sandwiches are favorites. Quintessentially Middle Eastern, falafel is fried balls of chickpeas mixed with garlic, onion, and spices. Falafel is usually served in pita bread, with tahini sauce (sesame seed paste) poured over the falafel.

Another dish enjoyed throughout Israel is *humus* (HOO-moos), a smooth paste of chickpeas with garlic and tahini sauce. Other Arabic foods that are quite popular among the people of Israel are *shawarma* (SHAH-wahr-mah), spicy sliced lamb or chicken usually served on pita; a marinated lamb dish called *shashlik* cooked on skewers over a flame; and shish kebab.

Cholent (CHOE-luhn) is a stew traditionally served on the Jewish sabbath, which is observed on Saturday. Because the oven in a religious home cannot be lit after sundown on Friday, cholent is a perfect meal. It simmers overnight in a warm oven turned on before the sabbath. Various types of cholent reflect the traditional foods of the different Jewish ethnic groups. Moroccan Jews, for example, use beef, spices, chickpeas, and potatoes, while Sephardic Jews include beans, meat, potatoes, and eggs.

Kugel (KOO-gehl), a noodle casserole that is a traditional food among Eastern European Jews, is also a sabbath favorite because it too can be left overnight in a warm oven and be ready for the meal on Saturday.

JEWISH DIETARY LAWS

Another factor that plays a significant role in the Israeli menu is the dietary laws of Jews and Muslims.

The *kashrut* is the kosher dietary system for Jews. Foods that are permitted are referred to as *kosher*, which means fit or proper. Those that are not are called *trefa* (treh-FAH). The dietary laws, which Jews have followed for thousands of years, are stated in the Bible and discussed extensively in the Talmud. Orthodox Jews believe that these laws are given by God and must not be violated.

Noodle kugel can be sweet or savory and is often served with brisket for holiday meals.

The kashrut falls into three categories: foods that can and cannot be eaten, the slaughter and preparation of meat, and the ways foods are served. (Since all kashrut rules involve animals, the Jewish vegetarian has little to worry about!)

The laws state that any animal with cloven or split hoofs that chews cud is edible; both criteria must be met. Therefore, lamb and beef are allowed, while rabbit, camel, and pork are not. Wild birds and birds of prey that seize food in their claws are unclean and therefore prohibited, but turkey, chicken, duck, and pigeon are fine. Fish that have fins and scales are clean and can be consumed, while those without, such as catfish, porpoise, shrimp, and lobster, are forbidden.

Animals and domestic fowl that can be eaten must be slaughtered and prepared according to strict rules that include removing the veins and arteries from the carcass. The meat must then be soaked in water and salted.

Rules for serving food state that dairy products and meat must not be eaten together. This separation is maintained throughout preparation, cooking, and eating, and separate sets of dishes, cookware, and silverware are required.

ISLAMIC DIETARY LAWS

Muslims also have dietary laws. Foods that are permitted are referred to as *halal* (hah-LULL). These laws are also about eating and slaughtering animals, and although they differ from the kashrut, they share some similarities. For example, consumption of blood and pork is prohibited. Food that is found dead or has been offered to idols is not edible for a Muslim and, as is the case with Jewish custom, animals must be slaughtered according to a ritual. Muslims are also prohibited from drinking alcohol.

HOLIDAY FOODS

All areas of Israeli life are influenced by the festivals and holy days of the Jewish year. So too are the foods eaten, because the festivals marking the holidays are usually observed by eating certain foods.

ROSH HASHANAH The Jewish year begins in autumn with Rosh Hashanah. Traditionally, sweet foods such as apples and honey are eaten to remind Jews of the sweetness of God's blessings. A round loaf of bread called *challah* (CHAH-lah) is also consumed. The round bread reminds Jews that they are bound to the wheel of fate. People eat pieces dipped in honey to ensure a sweet year. Salads and sour foods are avoided; nothing should alter the sweetness of the beginning of the year.

YOM KIPPUR takes place ten days after Rosh Hashanah. To atone for the sins of the past year, observant Jews eat no food from the hour before sunset on the eve of Yom Kippur until after sunset the next day. Bland chicken and rice is eaten before the fast to help prevent thirst and indigestion. Then a morsel of bread and water is taken as a symbolic gesture of nourishment. After the fast, families and friends eat together, starting with apple dipped in honey. Herring or other salty food follows. The rest of the meal consists of traditional foods of particular ethnic groups.

SUKKOT This eight-day harvest festival is marked by Orthodox Jews eating meals in the sukkah, a hut decorated with fruit which commemorates the huts that Jews lived in when they left Egypt and wandered in the desert for forty years before entering Israel. Harvest foods such as figs, apricots, pomegranates, onions, barley, and lettuce are part of each meal.

HANUKKAH The Festival of Lights is celebrated for eight days in the winter. It marks the time when a small amount of oil miraculously continued to burn in the rededicated temple in Jerusalem for eight days. Foods fried in oil, such as *latkes* (LAHT-kehs), or potato pancakes, and *sufganiyot* (soof-gah-ni-YOAT), or doughnuts, are enjoyed during this holiday.

PURIM Also known as the Feast of Esther, this springtime festival celebrates the story of Queen Esther saving the Jewish people from a murderous tyrant, Haman. People eat Haman's Ears, or *hamentashen* (HUH-muhn-tash), which are sweet cakes filled with prunes or poppy seeds. Wine is served, because Haman's defeat was due to the excessive amount of wine Esther served him. Traditional foods include chickpeas, *kreplach* (KREH-plah), or dumplings, and turkey.

PESACH, or Passover, celebrates the Jews' escape from Egypt. The fleeing Jews baked unleavened bread because they could not wait for the dough to rise. As a result, *matzo*, an unleavened cracker-like bread, is eaten. The first evening is marked by a ritual meal called a Seder, and for the remainder of the week, nothing leavened by yeast may be eaten. During the Seder, a special plate is prepared with foods recalling the trials of the Jews during the bitter years of Egyptian slavery. Foods include bitter herbs and hard-boiled eggs.

Ultra-Orthodox men inspect the *etorg*, or citrons, in a market. The thick-skinned citrus fruit is used in Sukkot celebrations and must meet a number of specifications.

SHAVUOT This holiday is the last festival of the year. It celebrates Moses receiving the Ten Commandments and the summer fruits coming into season. Dairy dishes such as cheese blintzes (pancakes) are served. Accompanying the milk products are honey biscuits to celebrate Israel being "the land of milk and honey."

SABBATH takes place on the seventh day of every week, starting at sundown Friday and ending at sundown Saturday. It is a special day of rest and prayer. Like all Jewish celebrations, the sabbath, or *shabat*, has its special foods, the most common being the challah, or sabbath bread. Each family has its own special dishes that are enjoyed on the sabbath.

STREET FOODS

Israelis are always on the move, and because there is not much leisure time, people like to eat and run. Israel not only has a lively street vendor industry, it also has a booming gas station/fast-food trade. What started out as a convenience—filling up the gas tank and stomach at the same time—has turned cultural. People dodge traffic to run and grab some *mezze* (MEH-zeh), an appetizer; grilled meat or fish; and sweet Turkish coffee.

For pedestrians, falafel is found almost everywhere. In fact, after paying for the first falafel on pita, Israelis can have additional servings of the chickpea mixture while only paying for the pita.

Another tasty street food is *brik*, which is filo dough filled with cheese or potato. Bagels are sold warm on street corners, and some vendors offer a tasty dip called za'atar (ZAH-ah-tahr). On the sweet side, a caramel-like custard called *malabi* (MAH-lah-bee) is eaten from little tin cups. *Tamarindi* (TAH-mah-reen-dee) is a favorite syrupy juice that street vendors carry in large jars on their shoulders. For fast food, hamburgers are available at MacDavid's, Israel's answer to McDonald's, and Burger Ranch. The similarities end there, however, because the hamburgers and hot dogs served in Israel are much spicier than those in the United States.

Perhaps the most common outdoor food is sunflower seeds. The experienced seed eater can remove the meat and spit out the shell without ever taking a hand to the mouth. Discarded shells line the sidewalks and roadways, signs that sunflower seeds are the ultimate street food in Israel.

FOOD SHOPPING

Although the supermarket concept is the same as in the United States, a quick glance at the shelves reveals that the goods on display are a little different from what is sold in North America. Milk, for example, comes in clear plastic sacks; dishwashing liquid is actually a yellow paste in a pail. Items that are available in the United States in many different brands and flavors, such as salad dressing, are available in Israel.

However, some Israelis never even go to the supermarket. In nearly every neighborhood there is a little grocery store known as a *makolet* (mah-KOH-let), which opens as early as 7 a.m. Usually family-owned, the makolet sells many things, from fresh rolls to dairy products, and a nice variety of sundries. There is a warm, friendly atmosphere at the makolet, and many choose to do their shopping in what is considered by some to be the neighborhood social center.

The open-air market, or *shuk*, is also a vital part of the Israeli shopping experience. Most towns have a shuk, where fruit and vegetables are offered at very reasonable prices. Vendors from all the stalls compete with one another, yelling the prices and benefits of their goods.

INTERNET LINKS

www.seriouseats.com/2012/07/snapshots-from-israel-best-things-i-ate-tel-aviv-jerusalem.html
Serious Eats: The 25 Best Things I Ate in Israel
A slideshow of iconic Israeli foods.

www.israelikitchen.com
Israeli Kitchen is a well-done food blog by an American in Israel.

BABA GANOUSH

This tasty eggplant dip is popular throughout the Middle East.

2 or 3 medium Italian eggplants
3 medium cloves of garlic, minced
Juice from 1 lemon, plus more as desired
⅓ cup of tahini
3 tablespoons extra-virgin olive oil,
  plus more for serving
¼ cup chopped fresh parsley leaves
Kosher salt, pepper

Preheat oven to 450°F. Rub the eggplants with olive oil and place them in a roasting pan. Roast the eggplant until the skin has charred and the interior is tender, 15 to 20 minutes. Let cool.

Peel and seed the cooled eggplant. Roughly chop the flesh, and then transfer it to the bowl of a food processor. Add the tahini, garlic, lemon juice, some salt and pepper to taste. Process the mixture until it becomes a coarse paste. Add cold water a little at a time if necessary to desired consistency. The mixture should become pale and creamy.

Transfer the baba ganoush to a bowl or serving dish. Drizzle with oil and sprinkle with parsley. Serve with extra lemon wedges and triangles of toasted pita bread. Baba ganoush can be stored in an airtight container in the refrigerator for up to four days. Let baba ganoush warm to room temperature before serving.

MALABI

This creamy rosewater-perfumed pudding is a favorite in Israel and other Middle Eastern countries.

4 cups milk, or a milk and cream combination

½ cup cornstarch

1 tablespoon rose water

½ teaspoon vanilla extract

⅓ cup sugar

Chopped pistachios or almonds for garnish

Raspberry or strawberry syrup (optional)

In a medium bowl, mix one cup of milk or cream with the cornstarch, rose water, and vanilla until the cornstarch dissolves; set aside. Bring remaining milk and sugar to a simmer in a saucepan over medium heat, stirring constantly. Watch that it doesn't boil over. Lower the heat, pour in the dissolved cornstarch mixture, and cook for a minute or two more, stirring constantly, until the mixture begins to thicken.

Remove from the stove and pour into serving dishes. Cover with plastic wrap and allow to cool to room temperature; then refrigerate for at least four hours. Serve topped with the chopped pistachios or almonds, and raspberry or strawberry syrup, if desired.

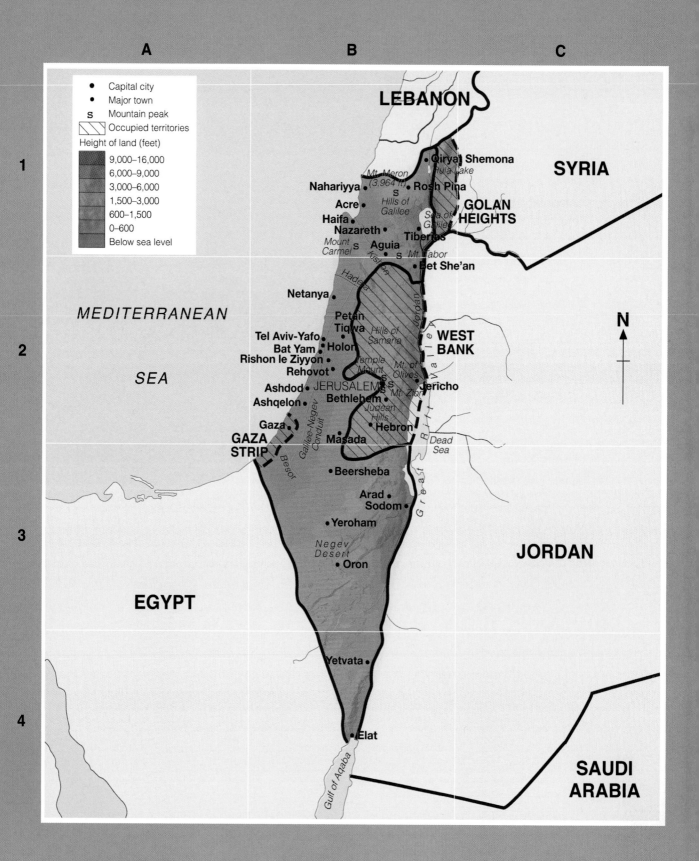

MAP OF ISRAEL

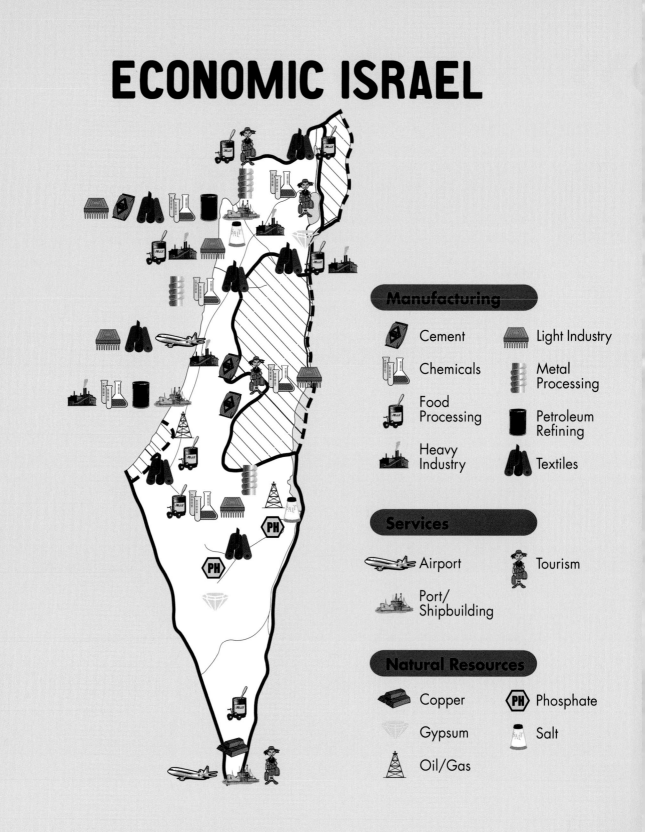

ECONOMIC ISRAEL

Manufacturing

- Cement
- Chemicals
- Food Processing
- Heavy Industry
- Light Industry
- Metal Processing
- Petroleum Refining
- Textiles

Services

- Airport
- Port/ Shipbuilding
- Tourism

Natural Resources

- Copper
- Gypsum
- Oil/Gas
- **PH** Phosphate
- Salt

ABOUT THE ECONOMY

OVERVIEW

Israel has a technologically advanced market economy. Between 2004 and 2011, growth averaged nearly 5 percent per year, although the economy suffered a downturn during the global financial crisis that began in 2008. Israel continues to have high rates of income inequality and poverty. Israel needs to bring more workers into its technology sector, which is where the future lies. The country also has to solve the problem of its fastest-growing but underemployed parts of society—the ultra-Orthodox and Arab communities.

GROSS DOMESTIC PRODUCT (GDP)

$274.5 billion (2013) US

CURRENCY

1 Israel new shekel (ILS) = 100 agorot
1 agora = 10 shekalim
1USD = 3.621 ILS (2013 est.)
Notes: 20, 50, 100, 200 new shekel
Coins: 1, 5, 10 agorot; 1/2, 1, 5, 10 shekalim

LABOR FORCE

3.606 million (2012)

UNEMPLOYMENT RATE

6.8 percent (2013)

INFLATION RATE

1.7 percent (2013)

LAND AREA

8,019.3 square miles (20,770 sq km)

LAND USE

Arable land: 13.68 percent
Permanent crops: 3.69 percent
Other: 82.62 percent (2011)

AGRICULTURAL PRODUCTS

Citrus fruits, vegetables, olives, cotton, beef, poultry, dairy products, fishing and aquaculture

MAJOR EXPORTS

Cut diamonds, medical equipment, software, scientific equipment, electronic components, apparel, computers, textiles, chemicals, agricultural products

MAJOR IMPORTS

Raw materials, military equipment, investment goods, rough diamonds, fuels, grain, consumer goods

MAJOR TRADE PARTNERS

U.S., 12.9 percent; China, 7.3 percent; Germany, 6.3 percent; Switzerland, 5.5 percent; Belgium, 4.8 percent (2012)

PORTS AND HARBORS

Ashdod, Eilat, Hadera, Haifa, Tel Aviv-Yafo

AIRPORTS

Ben Gurion, Ben Yaakov, Eilat-J Hozman, Haifa-U Michaeli, Sde Dov

TOURIST ARRIVALS

3.54 million tourist arrivals in 2013

CULTURAL ISRAEL

Baha'i Gardens
The holiest site of the Baha'i faith, in Haifa, marks the tomb of the founder of the faith, the prophet Baha'ullah.

Haifa Museums
Consists of three branches, including the Tikotin Museum of Japanese Art, the National Maritime Museum, and the Haifa Museum of Art.

Old Yafo
Ancient ruins stand alongside a modern urban area filled with galleries, shops, cafés, and restaurants in Tel Aviv-Jaffa.

Kikar Habimah
This major cultural center houses the Habimah National Theater, the Mann Auditorium (home of the Israeli Philharmonic Orchestra), the Helena Rubinstein Pavilion, and the Gan Ya'akov garden.

Tel Aviv Museum of Art
A world-renowned museum that houses Israeli and international art; known for its Impressionist and post-Impressionist collections.

Ruins of Masada
The mountaintop remains of the Roman king Herod's palace fortress in Masada. One thousand Jews committed mass suicide in their failed revolt against the Romans in 70 CE.

The Negev
The desert region houses craters, valleys, gorges, and mountains. Contains Makhtesh Ramon, the largest natural crater, and the Timna Mountains, where King Solomon mined copper.

Eilat (Red Sea)
The most popular tourist city in Israel, located near the sea in the southern tip of Israel.

The Western Wall
Part of the Second Temple complex built by Herod in Jerusalem, this is the retaining wall that was built around the Temple.

Dome of the Rock
An Islamic shrine built in 691 CE on the site of the First and Second Jewish Temples.

Church of the Holy Sepulcher
Christianity's holiest site was built in 330 CE and contains the location of Jesus' crucifixion, entombment, and resurrection.

El Aqsa Mosque
Islam's third most important place of worship, built in 720 CE.

Church of the Nativity
This church in Bethlehem marks Jesus' birthplace.

Dead Sea
This lake is the lowest place on Earth. The water is so salty that people can stay afloat without any effort.

Tomb of the Patriarchs
The tomb in Hebron is the burial site of Abraham, Isaac, and Jacob and their wives Sarah, Rebecca, and Leah.

The Bedouin Market
Held every Thursday in Beersheba, this market offers ethnic handicrafts such as embroidered clothing, rugs, camel bags, bracelets, amulets, beads, copperware, and coffee pots and mugs.

ABOUT THE CULTURE

OFFICIAL NAME
State of Israel.

DESCRIPTION OF NATIONAL FLAG
White with a blue hexagram (six-pointed linear star) known as the Magen David (Star of David or Shield of David) centered between two equal horizontal blue bands.

NATIONAL ANTHEM
"HaTikvah (*The Hope*)". Written in 1886 by Naftali Herz Imber. Adopted as the nation's anthem in 1948.

CAPITAL
Jerusalem.

OTHER MAJOR CITIES
Tel Aviv and Haifa.

POPULATION
7,821,850 (2014)
Note: approximately 341,400 Israeli settlers live in the West Bank (2012); approximately 18,900 Israeli settlers live in the Golan Heights (2012); approximately 196,400 Israeli settlers live in East Jerusalem (2011).

LITERACY RATE
97.1 percent.

ETHNIC GROUPS
Jewish, 75.1 percent (of which Israel-born, 73.6 percent); non-Jewish, 24.9 percent (mostly Arab) (2012).

RELIGIOUS GROUPS
Jewish, 75.1 percent; Muslim, 17.4 percent; Christian, 2 percent; Druze, 1.6 percent; other, 3.9 percent (2012).

OFFICIAL LANGUAGES
Hebrew is the official language; Arabic is used officially for the Arab minority.

NATIONAL HOLIDAYS
Independence Day. Israel declared independence on May 14, 1948, but following the Jewish lunar calendar, the holiday may fall in April or May.

LEADERS IN POLITICS
David Ben-Gurion—first prime minister (1948—54, 1955—63).
Golda Meir—prime minister (1969—74).
Yitzhak Rabin—prime minister (1974—77, 1992—96).
Shimon Peres—prime minister (1984—86, 1995—96).
Ariel Sharon—prime minister (2001—2006).
Shimon Peres—chief of state since 2007.
Benjamin Netanyahu—prime minister since 2009.

TIMELINE

IN ISRAEL	IN THE WORLD
13th century BCE Exodus from Egypt. Torah and the Ten Commandments received at Mount Sinai.	
722–720 BCE Assyrians exile ten Israeli tribes.	**753** BCE Rome is founded.
73 BCE Last stand of Jews at Masada.	**116–17** BCE The Roman Empire reaches its greatest extent, under Emperor Trajan (98–117).
	600 CE Height of Mayan civilization
	1000 The Chinese perfect gunpowder and begin to use it in warfare.
	1530 Beginning of trans-Atlantic slave trade organized by the Portuguese in Africa
	1558–1603 Reign of Elizabeth I of England
	1620 Pilgrims sail the *Mayflower* to America.
	1776 U.S. Declaration of Independence
	1789–99 French Revolution
1860 The first neighborhood, Mishkenot Sha'ananim, is built outside Jerusalem's walls.	**1861** U.S. Civil War begins.
	1869 The Suez Canal is opened.
1882–1903 First Aliyah, mainly from Russia	
1897 Zionist Organization is founded.	**1914** World War I begins.
1939–45 World War II; Holocaust in Europe	**1939** World War II begins.
1948 State of Israel is declared; Arab countries attack.	**1945** The United States drops atomic bombs on Hiroshima and Nagasaki.

IN ISRAEL	IN THE WORLD
1949 Egypt, Jordan, Syria, and Lebanon sign a ceasefire agreement. Israel becomes the 59th UN member.	**1949** North Atlantic Treaty Organization (NATO) is formed.
1952 Israel participates in the Olympic Games (in Helsinki) for the first time.	**1957** Russians launch Sputnik.
1967 Israel wins Six-Day War.	**1966–69** Chinese Cultural Revolution
1968–73 Egypt's War of Attrition against Israel	
1973 Yom Kippur War	
1978 Israel and Egypt sign Camp David Accords; Prime Minister Begin and Egyptian President Sadat win Nobel Peace Prize.	
1982 Israel invades Lebanon.	**1986** Nuclear power disaster at Chernobyl in Ukraine
1987 Intifada in Israel-administered areas	**1991** Break-up of the Soviet Union
1994 Israel pulls out from Jericho and Gaza and signs peace treaty with Jordan. Rabin, Peres, and Arafat win the Nobel Peace Prize.	
1995 Further Israeli withdrawals from the West Bank. Prime Minister Rabin is assassinated at a peace rally. Palestinian self-government widens in the West Bank and the Gaza Strip.	**1997** Britain returns Hong Kong to China. **2001** Terrorists crash planes in New York, Washington, D.C., and Pennsylvania.
2004 Yasser Arafat dies.	**2003** War in Iraq
2014 Former Israeli Prime Minister Ariel Sharon dies after eight years in a coma. Knesset votes that ultra-Orthodox Jews must serve in military.	**2013** South African leader Nelson Mandela dies.

GLOSSARY

aliyah (ah-lee-YUH)
Waves of Jewish immigrants to Israel; literally means *going up*

Ashkenazim (AHSH-kuh-NAH-zim)
Jews from northern and eastern Europe

diaspora
The dispersion of Jews after the Babylonian (587 BCE) and Roman (132 CE) conquests of Palestine

Histadrut (hiss-tahd-root)
The General Federation of Labor, Israel's most important workers' union

Holocaust
The killing of six million European Jews by the Nazis during World War II

Intifada (IN-tuh-FAH-duh)
Civil disobedience and unrest started in 1987 by Palestinian Arabs to protest Israeli occupation of the West Bank and the Gaza Strip

kibbutz (key-BOOTZ)
A collective farm where people work and live together, sharing all their possessions

kibbutznik (key-BOOTZ-nik)
Resident of the kibbutz

menorah (muh-noh-ruh)
The seven-branched candelabrum of traditional Jewish worship; the official Israeli emblem

Palestine
Historically, the area between the Jordan River and the Mediterranean Sea in which most of the biblical narrative is located

rabbi
A spiritual leader of a Jewish congregation

sabbath
The seventh day of the week (Saturday), set aside by the Fourth Commandment for rest and worship and observed as such by Jews

Sabra
Nickname for Israelis, derived from the name of a cactus fruit that is tough outside but sweet inside

Sephardim (suh-FAR-dim)
Jews from Aegean, Mediterranean, Balkan, and Middle Eastern countries

shofar (show-fahr)
A ram's horn, used in ancient times in religious ceremonies as a signal in battle

ulpan (ool-PAHN)
An institute specially designed to teach Jewish immigrants about the culture of Israel and to offer Hebrew-language lessons

Zionism
The effort of the Jews to regain and retain their biblical homeland, based on the promise in the Bible that Israel would belong to the Jews

FOR FURTHER INFORMATION

BOOKS

Abunimah, Ali. *The Battle for Justice in Palestine*. Chicago: Haymarket Books, 2014

Adwan, Sami and Dan Bar-On, Eyal Naveh (editors). *Side by Side: Parallel Histories of Israel-Palestine*. New York: New Press, 2012.

Ansky, Sherry and Nelli Sheffer. *The Food of Israel: Authentic Recipes from the Land of Milk and Honey (Food of the World Cookbooks)*. Periplus Editions, 2000.

Aronson, Marc. *Unsettled: The Problem of Loving Israel*. New York: Atheneum Books for Young Readers, 2010.

Barakat, Ibtisam. *Tasting the Sky: A Palestinian Childhood*. Farrar, Straus and Giroux, (YA fiction), 2007.

Bard, Mitchell G. *Myths and Facts: A Guide to the Arab-Israeli Conflict*. Chevy Chase: American-Israeli Cooperative Enterprise (AICE), 2011.

DK Eyewitness Travel Guide. *Jerusalem, Israel, Petra & Sinai*. London: DK Publishing, 2012.

Ehrlich, Amy and David Nevins (illustrator). *With a Mighty Hand: The Story in the Torah*. Somerville: Candlewick Press, 2013

Immell, Myra. *Israel (Opposing Viewpoints)* Farmington Hills: Greenhaven Press, 2011.

Laird, Elizabeth and Sonia Nimr. *A Little Piece of Ground*. Chicago: Haymarket Books, 2006.

Shavit, Ari. *My Promised Land*. New York: Spiegel & Grau, 2013.

Zenatti, Valerie. *When I Was a Soldier*. New York: Bloomsbury USA Childrens, 2007

_____. *A Bottle in the Gaza Sea*. New York: Bloomsbury USA Childrens, (YA fiction), 2008

DVDS/FILMS

5 Broken Cameras. Kino Lorber, 2011

50 Years War: Israel & The Arabs. PBS Home Video, 2000

Israel: A Nation Is Born. Home Vision Entertainment, 2002

Israel: The Royal Tour. PBS, 2014

Jerusalem: Center of the World. PBS, 2009

WEBSITES

BBC News. "A History of Conflict." http://news.bbc.co.uk/2/shared/spl/hi/middle_east/03/v3_ip_timeline/html

Ha'aretz Daily Newspaper (English-language version). www.haaretzdaily.com

Israeli government official site. www.knesset.gov.il

Jerusalem Post (English-language newspaper). www.jpost.com

BIBLIOGRAPHY

BOOKS

Eban, Abba. *Personal Witness: Israel Through My Eyes*. New York: G.P. Putnam's Sons, 1992

Grossman, David. *Sleeping on a Wire: Conversations with Palestinians in Israel*. New York: Farrar, Straus and Giroux, 1993

Harper, Paul. *The Arab-Israeli Conflict*. New York: Bookwright Press, 1990

Metz, Helen Chapin (editor). *Israel, a Country Study*. Washington, D.C.: U.S. Government Printing Office, 1990

Reich, Bernard and Gershon Kieval. *Israel, Land of Tradition and Conflict*. Boulder, CO: Westview Press, 1993.

Winter, Dick. *Culture Shock! Israel*. Portland, OR: Graphic Arts, 1992.

WEBSITES

BBC News. "History of Israel: Key Events." http://news.bbc.co.uk/2/hi/middle_east/7385661.stm

B'Tselem—The Israeli Information Center for Human Rights in the Occupied Territories. www.btselem.org

Central Intelligence Agency World Factbook/Israel. www.cia.gov/cia/publications/factbook/geos/is.html

Economist. Israel section. www.economist.com/countries/Israel

Embassy of Israel in Washington, D.C. www.israelemb.org

Fodors. Travel guide. www.fodors.com

Frommers. Travel guide. www.frommers.com

History.com. "Yom Kippur War." A&E Networks, 2009. www.history.com/topics/yom-kippur-war/israel_and_the_palestinian_territories

Israel Ministry of Foreign Affairs. www.israel-mfa.gov.il

Israel Ministry of Tourism. www.goisrael.com

Jewish Virtual Library. www.jewishvirtuallibrary.org

Jimmy Carter Library. "The Camp David Accords." 1978. www.jimmycarterlibrary.gov/documents/campdavid/frame.phtml

Library of Congress. "Israel, a country study." http://lcweb2.loc.gov/frd/cs/iltoc.html

Lonely Planet. "Israel and the Palestinian territories." www.lonelyplanet.com/destinations/middle_east

Ministry of Agriculture. "Israel's Agriculture." 2010. www.moag.gov.il/agri/files/Israel's_Agriculture_Booklet.pdf

My Jewish Learning. www.myjewishlearning.com

State of Israel. www.stateofisrael.com

Virtual Jerusalem. www.virtualjerusalem.com

INDEX

INDEX